THE UNTOLD SECRETS TO HEALING

DISCOVER THE POWER OF NATURAL HEALING AND BEGIN YOUR TRANSFORMATION OF THE MIND, BODY AND SOUL. *** AN EDUCATIONAL GUIDE ON HOW TO RECOVER FROM ILLNESS AND THE ADVERSE EFFECTS OF THE COVID VACCINE. *** A HOLISTIC JOURNEY TO TOTAL HEALTH AND WELLNESS, BACKED BY THE SCIENCE OF ALTERNATIVE MEDICINE.

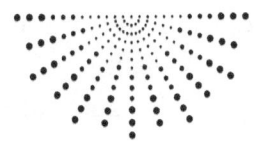

SKYE ANGELOU

CONTENTS

FORWARD

"**If you think you can, or you think you can't, you are right.**"

— ABRAHAM LINCOLN

If you are ready to break through the barricades of lies and old conditioning, then this book is your first step to discovering a new way of healing. For decades we have been lied to by the healthcare system we trusted and depended on so much. I know this is difficult to hear, especially if you are someone who still suffers. However, this book will open your eyes to the truth. Dare I say it, but the time has come that you are educated and know what is standing in the way of your health and healing.

This book will show you the other side of health and wellness, including exciting possibilities and resources within your reach. It is time to heal.

Unlock the secret to transforming your well-being and *tap into your hidden healing powers* **with this groundbreaking guide.**

Beautifully written with authentic advice, personal anecdotes, and timeless spiritual wisdom, this illuminating book combines modern scientific insights with **traditional healing wisdom** to provide readers with a blueprint for *taking their health into their own hands.*

Specially written for anybody suffering from health conditions or chronic illnesses that modern medicine can't seem to cure, or if you're curious about unlocking your hidden healing powers, this profound guide offers a **paradigm-shifting approach that redefines the way you look at well-being.**

With fascinating lessons that reveal the immense power we have to heal our own bodies, this book empowers readers of all backgrounds to overcome the shortfalls of Western medicine and approach their health in a life-affirming new way.

Here's just a little of what you'll discover inside:

- The Secret Way That Anybody Can Heal Themselves – No Matter Your Age, Background, or Condition
- Exploring The Hidden Root Causes of Most Modern Illnesses (and Why Western Medicine Can't Seem To Fix Them)
- A Groundbreaking New Approach To Personal well-being and Holistic Healing The Not-So-Secret Killers in The Modern World – and How We Can Stop Them From Shaving Years Off Our Lives
- Practical Strategies For Transforming Your Health, From Stress Management and Emotional Support to Lifestyle and Dietary Changes
- And Much More...

Packed with tried-and-tested strategies, straightforward advice, and heartfelt guidance, *The Untold Secrets to Healing* inspires you to stop relying on doctors and start taking an active role in your well-being.

After reading this book, we have a special offer for you or your loved ones. So get ready for information that will change how you view your body, health, and wellness.

PREFACE

Some things in life are so simple and yet so mysterious. We all struggle to find answers. It's something that we all share as part of the human experience.

Truth is a rare commodity. Lies are plentiful and profitable to those that peddle them. There's just no money in truth it seems. So, not many people are willing to be truthful and transparent.

Even really good people will reserve key information so that they may profit in some way over those that lack the knowledge and skills necessary. This paradigm has radically shaped our reality to a large extent and it is a big blockage for humanity.

People suffer and die needlessly from lack of knowledge. Take all the children that suffer from cancer and other illnesses, when if parents only knew there is another way. It's not always due to a lack of trying on their part. The water is just so murky. How can one possibly find the truth? You read one thing and it sounds good. Then you read something else and it contradicts the first thing. The more you dig and research, the more confusing it can get. Add in censorship, propaganda and influencer profiteering into the mix and it becomes very difficult to find the actual truth about healing yourself or your loved one.

Discernment is a hot word these days. But how do you do it? How does someone discern what is true and what they should do? Trust is a big issue. When we lose trust in others, we can lose trust in ourselves. Many people have also lost trust in God, source, creator, universal energy, or whatever name you want to give it.

If you suffer from pain, disease or illness and haven't found answers from traditional sources, then you must look beyond. You cannot give up hope, unless you want to stay sick. There is no judgement either way. Help doesn't come to those who don't help themselves.

This book will give you a new perspective in your healing journey. It is not for everyone, but if you are genuinely seeking to step outside the box of your current reality into a new one, you choose your outcome. We have more control in our healing than we know.

Disclaimer

In no way does this book discredit modern medicine or capabilities to help people heal. However, modern medicine should never be your first and only option for you or a loved one. What will it take to try something new? This book will give you a deep perspective on your health and healing.

ACKNOWLEDGMENTS

- To those who have suffered far too long before finding the root cause.
- To the brave who are open to alternative methods to heal themselves once and for all. To those doctors, nurses and coroners who bravely and courageously spoke out about the truth about the pandemic and vaccinations.
- To anyone still struggling with their disease or illness, do not give up. There is hope, and possibly the reason you have found this book.
- To my Guardian Angel for always protecting me. You know who you are. I love you.
- To my mom & dad for always telling me I could do anything I put my mind to.
- To my mother, who passed from cancer before I knew the healing modalities that I have discovered. Her strength and

positive attitude will always be remembered.

- To my children for being so patient and understanding while I often had to be away from them to help those in need. You are my life and my love.
- To my aunt for inspiring me toward natural healing at such a young age.
- To those who left this planet early, those who suffered and didn't get to have the quality of life here on earth.
- We all deserve to live a life without suffering. May we be able to put an end to unnecessary suffering and bring eternal joy into our lives! You deserve perfect health. It is achievable for all.

INTRODUCTION

"Time and health are two precious assets that we don't recognize and appreciate until they have been depleted."

— DENIS WAITLEY

After reading this book, you will think differently about your health and ability to heal. What I am about to share, is not all positive. If you are reading this, then I would say you're ready for the truth and a good dose of reality. Much has been held from you, so you haven't been able to heal. Healing uses the power of the mind, under-standing energy, natural remedies and advanced modalities that existed long before prescription medications and surgery.

I learned the power of energy and natural healing at a young age and witnessed the miracles my aunt performed to save the lives of her son and her mother, (my grandmother). Learning about energy taught me to recover from stage 4 cancer and to never get sick again. I can honestly say that other than a slight cold, I've never been ill.

Your ability to heal is independent of how good your doctor is and the type of medication you receive, or the surgery you get. It is not the disease or illness you might suffer from, or the "expiration date" your doctor may have assigned to you. It is not how healthy or unhealthy you've been in the past or what the medical prognosis for your future health looks like.

It is the elephant in the room that has become impossible to ignore. People in the US are arguably sicker than ever before. Yet western medicine is touted as the best in the world. However, other countries encompass an impressive complement of cutting-edge technologies and modalities, while many of our hospitals and clinics still need to be updated.

As a nationally recognized provider of natural and advanced holistic treatments and technologies, I have dedicated my life to learning about energy healing and empowering others to heal themselves. I have helped thousands around the world restore their health. I continually travel the globe, meeting other healers, alternative health providers, doctors, and scientists gathering information on some of the newest successful, proven, scientific healing technologies. Many of these have been banned, lost, hidden, kept secret, or underground, especially in the United States.

Your instinct may be to discount what I say because I am not a doctor, nor do I have a degree in medicine. But after 30 plus years of experience, I have helped thousands of people facilitate their own healing regardless of age, condition, or location through our advanced holistic methods. Please reflect on your reactions to the information I share. When we react negatively to new ideas, it is often fear-based.

We must push past those initial fear-based reactions and dare to explore the possibility that alternative medicine will be the future of healing. When introduced to new ideas, especially ones that challenge your perspective, research is paramount. Don't simply rely on what someone else tells you. We tend to believe information that aligns with our personal views and values.

Remember, we mentioned the human body consists of energy that can be used to heal any disease. Regardless of your political, religious, physical, or vocational identity and views, being open-minded and willing to evolve has never been more crucial to humans than now. After all, what is the alternative? If you need an example of the importance of evolution, look at any species in nature. What happens when something stops evolving? It becomes extinct.

There are spectacular natural healing technologies and modalities available today. They enable us to completely heal ourselves and effectively from any illness. I've devoted my life to understanding these principals and sharing it with others. If "seeing is believing," then my wish is for you to experience the miracle of healing for yourself.

At the end of this book, I want you to always remember one fact. When you are aware of a problem, then the solution becomes easy.

"A healer's power stems not from any special ability, but from maintaining the courage and awareness to embody and express the universal healing power that every human being naturally possesses."

— ERIC MICHAEL LEVENTHAL

HEALTH IS WEALTH

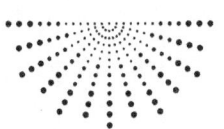

"Health is more than the absence of disease. Health is about all the things that go into making us healthy."

— JOYCELYN ELDERS

*H*ealth is wealth. Haven't we heard this a thousand times? Do you truly know what it signifies? It means no matter how much wealth you have, without health, you have nothing. Wealth is pointless if you don't have the health to enjoy it. Wealth may give you an advantage; say for better medical care to some degree. But known wealthy icons like Michael Jackson or Steve Jobs couldn't even save their lives with all the money they had. Knowledge will be the wealth needed for your health.

The world, unfortunately, has been draped in dark clothing for ages regarding the options available for health, healing, and wellness. Let me ask you a simple question. Would understanding the under- lying issues of your health make any difference in your life? Would you do something about it? Would it make you be more confident in overcoming it? Would you seek out treatments to address it? After all, here in America, we are used to our doctors simply prescribing medications and surgery, rather than addressing the root cause.

If you knew the end of days or how long to pro-long it, would you spend more time to do the things you love? Would you spend time with those you love and care for? Would you create happier memories and avoid the negative experi-ences that come your way? Before you answer, how aware are you of alternative medicine or the potency of natural and holistic methods?

When was the last time you experienced pain? Maybe it was a terrible migraine, breaking your leg, or losing a loved one. When we lose a partner, child, or friend, we suffer the most intense emotions apart from our own death. Suffering from mental, emotional, spiritual, or physical pain can be unbearable. Nothing matters at that point, does it? Were you able to focus or even care about anything other than relieving or numbing your pain? Everything of importance has now become less enticing. That new dress you were going to wear for your anniversary, the new car you wanted to buy, or the new job position you were going to apply for...none of it matters anymore. Quality of life starts with feeling good.

Pain and suffering is a message that something is out of place or out of balance. Whether it is experienced in our mind or in our bodies, you are not alone. Such suffering is experienced by millions across the globe. If you have experienced such pain, it is a wake-up call to never take your health for granted.

Personally, I take 60 seconds every morning to be grateful and acknowledge being healthy before I open my eyes and get out of bed. I have had times where I suffered from pain and it even lasted for years. There is a way out. There is hope. There is healing waiting for you. You just need to know what you don't know.

Everyone deserves quality of life, and everyone deserves perfect health. Our brains and our bodies want to heal. Our brains and our bodies are designed to heal. Nothing should get in the way of your healing, especially money. Regardless of whether you are rich or poor, your health is paramount. Without our health, we have nothing. Nothing is more fulfilling than the feeling of total wellness. Without health, it's pretty impossible to hold a job, be in a relationship or feel that you are living the best part of your life.

When we feel healthy, strong, and vibrant, we are physically able to do whatever we want. When our health begins to suffer, everything in our life begins to deteriorate. True happiness lies within us and not in our worldly possessions. When we die, there is nothing we can take with us, not even the memories we hold in our mind. Genuine happiness comes from living in the present moment. Feeling good is to feel God.

If you are suffering, if possible try to direct your attention away from your problems and focus on helping someone else's pain. That act alone is healing ourselves.

To me, nothing is as fulfilling as helping others heal and get their lives back. Changing and saving other people's lives regardless of their mental, spiritual, or physical issues is truly miraculous. I would never believe what I do if I didn't see the results people have on a daily basis. Assisting people to become healthier is the greatest gift you can give to another. There is no good deed higher than that. It becomes so rewarding and fulfilling that nothing else matters except to help facilitate the blessing of being healthy for those less fortunate. Perhaps that is why I have been so healthy all my life. This is my path, my journey and I am just a vessel in which our Devine Creator works through. I focus on the needs of others and my needs are met, always.

"Live each day."

— JEFF V.

2

FEAR WILL KILL YOU

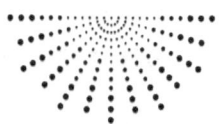

"Fear defeats more people than any other one thing in the world."

— RALPH WALDO EMERSON

ear will Kill You. Today, we face a pandemic of misinformation dubbed "fake news." In this era of information abundance, we must be vigilant with the data we integrate into our lives and guard ourselves against anything that prevents us from moving forward, because of fear. Don't be afraid to ask questions, seek alternative viewpoints, and continue challenging old perceptions that no longer serve you.

Intuition is our best defense from fear. Fear shouldn't lead you to panic . People panic because lack of something, like money, oxygen, time, resources, etc. What are you lacking?

It might sound surprising, but fear will kill you faster than any illness. Fear is one of our most basic human emotions. Ultimately, the fundamental purpose of fear is to keep us alive. When your brain perceives danger, it triggers a fear response.

Two great stories, both are true...Where I grew up there were tornados that swept the countryside every year. One farmer built an underground bunker to protect himself in the event of a tornado. The very next tornado that rolled through, he was nowhere near his bunker when the tornado hit and he died. That was an eye opener for me a child because I saw that you cannot escape death when it is your time to go. Funny thing was, nobody else died and nor did they have bunkers.

Another time when I was living in Chicago, my neighbor in my next apartment on the 35th floor was quite the hypochondriac. No judgement or anything but he was afraid of everything. He didn't fly as he was afraid of planes, afraid to drive, afraid to take a taxi, etc. A couple of years rolled by, and he told me about how his daughter was graduating. He was going to make the sacrifice to leave his home to see her graduate college. Walking was his only way of feeling safest from something happening to him.

Well, low and behold, not 4 blocks from his home, a pane of glass fell from a high-rise building and struck him in the head. He was dead on contact.

These are two significant memories of real life encounters. What you think about, you bring about. So be careful to not hold fear because you will attract more of that.

In contrast, I traveled the world during COVID-19. I never got sick and had the time of my life. I had no fear of anything going wrong, and it didn't.

First let's understand the difference between fake and phantom fear. Phantom fear is when you are flying on an airplane and some turbulence occurs and you are afraid you are going to crash and die.

You breakout in a sweat, your heart is pounding while tightly gripping the chair.

By breaking down the facts and logic of this phantom fear you are experiencing, your fear will reduce and perhaps leave altogether. Realizing that planes crash far less than automobiles and planes are designed to handle extreme turbulence. In fact, planes don't crash because of turbulence, but of other things like no fuel, engine failure, pilot dies from his COVID-19 vaccination, etc.

Real fear is when you are looking down the barrel of a gun pointed at your head by your killer after he just threw you into the back of his trunk. You have my full permission to be afraid and react accordingly.

We have all had moments where we see something lurking in the dark, while unaware (as in cannot see it), we only imagine the worst. As a human, the negative thoughts come flooding in. You see a figure of a person, and then your mind projects it as a burglar. You are frozen by fear and a million and one thoughts race through your mind. You think of escape routes, what is this person doing in your home! How you will react?

What if you had a gun or a knife? The thoughts keep coming. How are you going to fight them, keep it from harming you or escaping the danger it poses?

However, you waited for seconds and minutes, and as more light floods the room, it was just a pile of clothes you forgot to put away piled on a chair. But you were immobilized by fear as your hormones raged and your heart pounded. Not knowing the truth almost gave you a heart attack!

Remember, I did say that ONE of the take aways from this book is the hidden secrets that are kept away from us. This story is just like it.

The irony is many people are here and being tormented by fear. It is a negative emotion and reaction and only blooms when we allow it. While it is a part of life and the consciousness of the mind, it is detrimental to our overall well-being, wellness, and health.

However, when we face the fear we feel, by gaining knowledge, asking questions, and trying out new (or old) treatments when we are ill, we can cast fear aside and receive total healing. We must step aside from the things we have grown accustomed to when it is no longer working. As the saying goes, leave when the ovation is loudest.

Fear magnifies issues, but knowledge and awareness dissipates it and gives us power. We need to know when we are not in control and then take it back.

I have often witnessed clients filled with fear that they have made their health worse to the point of dying. Some clients are so afraid of which path is going to heal them, they bounce from one to another and therefore nothing works.

Some clients were so fearful of COVID-19, rather than staying healthy and keeping their immune system strong, they went and got vaccinated which only lowers the immune system, causing them to get COVID-19 multiple times or seeing their health issue magnify. Or wearing masks, that even the CDC said they didn't prevent the spread of COVID-19.

Eliminating fear mentally is essential. The body goes were the brain goes. If the brain or mind is thinking I am going to get sick, then the cells feel that and respond accordingly. What you think about you bring about.

Fear is unhealthy and detrimental to our well-being and growth. How fear overrides our mental senses is impressive, but are you aware that anxiety can cause imbalances in your energy levels? Yes, it can. We are all filled with the life force energy that ensures our physical, emotional, and spiritual bodies work in harmony. Many of us fall sick and experience one or another for two reasons. One, there is no harmony between the mind, body, and spirit.

Two, there is a hindrance to the flow of this life force across our bodies. However, if an external force disrupts the harmony, we become imbalanced, confused, disconnected, stagnant, and hidden.

Living in fear is baseless and causes an imbalance of life force energy that scatters our body's central harmony point. The result is a physical manifestation such as disease, emotional expressions such as stress, anxiety, or another mental ailment, or a spiritual image like narrow-mindedness and hatred for life.

If you are confused about life force energy, let's look at it from another perspective. Imagine your life like a river, like the Euphrates River that flows from the Garden of Eden. It is your life force energy that flows unhindered all over your body. Now imagine interrupting this flow with fear. The flow shifts from its initial route and creates other tributaries, causing an imbalance. What do you think happens?

If you allow the fear to continue, the imbalance deepens, creating more problems. For example, sudden fear can cause your heart to beat faster, but if calmness follows, you are good to go. However, if you allow the fear to continue, you suddenly feel your head pounding, shortness of breath, incapacitation, and mental health degradation.

All this happens from one could-have-been-avoided issue. If the case were different, you would become well again. Fear not only creates this imbalance, but lowers the power of your life force energy, making you susceptible to diseases.

Alarm Phase

When we experience an external factor that triggers fear, our bodies react in specific ways. Stress hormones such as adrenaline and cortisol are released in your body, making you feel the need to act in self-defense or flee. It is the alarm phase.

You are scared of present danger and prepare to deal with it. For example, if you were walking down the street and spotted a car barreling toward you out of control. What will your response be? You probably would jump out of the way. That response probably just saved your life. However, it is only sometimes like that. Sometimes our brain perceives danger in situations that challenge our personal beliefs and opinions.

Many of us will ignore ideas that threaten our worldview until we cannot ignore them, or it becomes a norm. When we can no longer ignore them, we may reject or dismiss them because we don't understand them or continue with the ignoring tactic.

Resistance Phase

At this point, we are in the resistance phase, where we think we understand it, and our body accepts it and works around this thought. Most people will notice a renewal or acceptance taking place in you. Although it feels good, it reduces our defense and weakens our life force energy. For example, when events challenge our perception, we get angry. But when you drill down, you often find fear at the root of your response. Your brain can misinterpret situations it does not understand as being dangerous, triggering that fear response.

Exhaustion Phase

The third stage is the exhaustion phase, where a particular action has continued for severally, and you are tired and care less about the consequences. For example, the vaccinations forced upon people during the COVID-19 Pandemic. Many people deceitfully believed this would prevent them from getting the virus. In hindsight, those are the same people who got it repeatedly. Why? It weakened their immune systems. What is worse?

But in non-life-threatening situations, fear is a self-limiting emotion. However, we remained afraid of limiting information or truths and contradictions— the vaccinations harm us, not protect us. Depopulation is a real thing. What you have yet to hear is how to increase your immune system as a natural way for the body to defend itself. Even research shows vitamin D helps boost one's immunity. Fear prevented that for us when we stayed indoors.

Oxygen is a known fact to keep us healthy, but how can we get our required oxygen if we wear a mask everywhere?

My wellness center exploded during COVID-19 but has escalated with vaccine-injured men, women, and children. Those with known or unknown issues escalated. Clients suffer mentally and emotionally because they have witnessed the deaths of many family and friends of sudden and mysterious deaths. It will continue to worsen as the life expectancy after the vaccination is 3 months to 6 years.

However, there is nothing to fear because there are ways to detox from these poisons. Again, this comes with knowledge to help you not be afraid but help your heal.

"WE DO no fear the unknown. We fear what we think we know about the unknown."

— TEAL SWAN

WHY IS FEAR detrimental to your health?

Let's not get this fear thing twisted. Scientifically, fear adversely affects the biochemical state of your body by lowering your immune system and increasing your risk of being infected and falling sick. The human body has diseases causing bacteria in our body, but when we are healthy, and our energy is balanced, we suppress the power of pathogens to cause harm. However, when an external force like fear offsets our balance, the energy vibrations are affected, lowering and making us prone to diseases.

FEAR DAMAGES OUR CARDIOVASCULAR SYSTEM.

It is the body's way of dealing with fright. When we scare, the first signs are an intense tightness in the chest region, quickened heartbeat, and circulation spontaneously. The result is adrenaline pumped into the bloodstream leading to tissue damage, blood vessel constriction, and high blood pressure. Young people might get away with the immediate and long term danger of this. However, seniors can suffer deadly heart-related conditions such as arrhythmia and irregular blood circulation. In severe cases, patients can drop dead from fear due to takotsubo syndrome (when the heart is too weak to pump blood). Remember, fear is overexertion of the vessels, arteries, and muscles. If you are not fit, any imbalance is detrimental.

Fear shuts your thinking capacity and capability.

When we fear, stress hormones flood our bodies and interfere with our ability to be rational. In this heightened state, we perceive every event around the circumstance as dangerous, and our emotions go haywire. In fact, in such a situation, our sense organs produce whack results which can increase the fear impact on us. Being aware of a fearful situation for a long can etch such events in our heads. For example, a veteran soldier from a war can unconsciously suffer fear bouts from seeing or hearing details likened to actions at the war front. These fear tendencies result from their negative impact on the hippocampus section of the brain, which is an ability to regulate emotions like fear itself. It ultimately affects mental health, causing depression, anxiety, or PTSD.

. . .

FEAR WEAKENS THE IMMUNE SYSTEM.

When we encounter fear, cortisol is released, and we experience stress which weakens the immune system as the number of lymphocytes in circulation reduces in the body. This process weakens the immune system and makes us susceptible to infection.

The lymphocytes are our defense mechanism to ensure pathogens do not get a field day, but fear incapacitates them and their ability to create a counter-invasion during an infection. Another reason is that fear triggers the body to shut down organs or systems it does not need immediately, as it envisions a flight, freeze, or fright mode. Finally, the gut is one such system, and the immune system resides within it.

FEAR CAUSES CHRONIC HEALTH ISSUES.

Fear is an aggravator that escalates minor issues into major problems. Constantly being in a state of fear has been shown to cause several health issues, including gastrointestinal ulcers, irritable bowel syndrome, decreased chances of fertility, fatigue, wrinkles, and mental weakness.

Fear is a lower energy, and what you fear most is what you attract into your life more. When you harbor fear for whatever reason, there are several ways to restore your energy balance and help you live a fulfilling life.

There is what you know. This is what you don't know and there is what you don't know that you don't know. I am helping you with what you don't know, that you don't know.

I am not a conspiracy theorist. Anyone who might suggest anything outside of mainstream media gets blamed of being such. I say it is healthy to look at all things and consider them. Have an open mind, do you research and consider the sources of your information. Mainstream media like NBC, ABC, FOX, etc. are all tied in with the same corrupt people as Big Pharma and our government.

I am going to share a little more with you, based on fact. Fact that I have a system, very advanced, more advanced than what is available in western medicine hospitals and clinics.

Without the advanced technology we have at our wellness center, we would not know the horrendous cocktails inside these vaccines. I became suspicious after vaccinated clients presented with cancer and HIV. Remember those healed and reversed just as they were back in the 1900s. But what about the thousands of people walking around not knowing they even have it? A vast awakening is upon us. We need to STOP being afraid, stop living in fear, stop following the fake news and lies, and wake up, or this evil will defeat us.

Fear and emotions are types of measurable energies. Fear is a lower vibrational energy we feel and so do our cells. We begin to resonate with that lower energy, and guess what? We are making ourselves even weaker! It is only going to make us sicker. Fear causes stress and stress is the number one cause of disease and illness.

Stop living in fear. Eliminate your fear and begin to trust in your higher power. Tap into your higher self to see and feel the truth and let that guide you. Trust it and have faith.

> **"Everything you have ever wanted, is sitting on the other side of fear."**
>
> — GEORGE ADDAIR

3

THE TRUTH ABOUT OUR HEALTHCARE SYSTEM: PERCEPTION VS. REALITY

"Perception is like painting scenery - no matter how beautifully you paint, it will still be a painting of the scenery, not the scenery itself."

The government regulates our healthcare system here in America. Big Pharma, (the pharmaceutical industry) and our government have been working together for years. They control the system, and our health! As Americans, we are not aware of the corrupt acts and dealings it has on us and our loved ones.

The number one question I get from clients after they heal from their disease or illness is...

"Why doesn't the whole world know about your healing methods?"

Then I explain, successfully helping people heal, is a threat to Big Pharma and our government. Those who dare to stand in the way of this are threatened and literally killed, covered up like a suicide. By keeping people sick, the more medications and surgeries will continue to profit. There is no money is healthy people!

Why does the government have so much interest in the healthcare sector? It's all about control, greed and money. Sadly many medical professionals are paid and/or controlled by the system to keep these evil, corrupt practices going so that Big Pharma and government can reap billions while keeping us sick!

If you really want to dig, you will see that everything, and I do mean everything is owned by two powerful companies, Vanguard and Blackrock. A few elites rule the world, while our government is supported by pharmaceutical companies. The clampdown on alternative medicine and proven cures for diseases like AIDS, Cancers, Alzheimer's, is harsh, even though they know it can be a vital contributor to the healthcare industry to save lives. But that is not what they want.

So much truth is leaking out, so I am obliged to prepare you for what you will soon be hearing. You may be in the know, but millions are unaware of this truth and choose to ignore it or will not address it. As my daughter says, ignorance is bliss, and while I What does it hurt to just see another perspective? Knowledge is power and it is time to take back our power. Go to WEFreport s.com, Listen to Whitney Webb.

Today in fact, I spoke with the sister, who held the executive decisions for her brother's health. He had a stroke. He wants our help as we have helped hundreds of stroke victims come out of a coma, speak, come out of paralysis, etc. We have successfully facilitated stroke victims back to a better quality of life. Helping them recover from coma's, paralysis, walking, talking and more.

When talking to the sister, she doesn't know or understand our world of advanced alternative healing. The unknown causes fear, so she condemns it, fears it and won't allow it. Thank God he is of sound mind and made the decision to back his power of attorney. But still, we face another problem.

The nursing home or care facility be is in, creates another barrier. Not only do they not want to be held liable for something going wrong, but the real issue would be if something actually went right! That would mean they lose money!

Even at the request of the patient, the facility will not allow food, healthy supplements and even natural modalities such as light therapy to be used by their patient. It is unbelievable and sad. Here is this guy who has hope, an open mind and has the money but literally cannot do anything because his sister controls his destiny and so does the facility. Who loves and cares about him? Certainly not his sister and the care facility.

Before we run ahead, let's understand how perception distorts our reality. We all have different perceptions of life and the barrage of things that come with it. While perceiving is not necessarily wrong, at what point did it become an acceptable reality?

We see the world as "they" want us to see it. Whether it is the entertainment industry, fashion industry, or us or the healthcare sector and the government, we have based our reality on our background, beliefs, past experiences, emotions, hurts, and layers or layers of unreal circumstances. This biased view is detrimental and continues to destroy our reality. That is, if we even understand it.

Big Pharma & our government continues to do everything to keep us sick. That is what power does. As long as healthcare is a body we all depend on to survive, it can be used to continue feeding our minds and keeping us in the dark about alternatives that will take money and control from their hands.

The pharmaceutical industry controls our healthcare system, and the underlining motivating factor is money, not to help people to heal! It is corrupt and regarded as a business to make money rather than help people heal. I do not blame medical professionals such as doctors and nurses. They are pawns in the hands of the top elites. Many doctors know how bad the vaccinations are but they still are ordered to push it on people.

Even universities and schools are paid vast sums of money to push the poisonous shots to our children when thousands of kids are dying? Where is our freedom of choice? Where have our rights gone?

The truth is bitter, and while doctors and medical practitioners are under a strict oath to be 100% honest with their patients, could they be playing a double role and tempted to lie to satisfy Big Pharma and the government to your detriment?

Take for instance a client of mine who was told she had to have her bladder removed because it was full of cancer. She was sobbing as she described what her life was going to be, carrying a bag around to drain her urine repeatedly. I advised she get a scan so we could see the situation.

We ran our bio-resonance scan, which is very accurate and it didn't show any cancer. It did show a few benign cysts. With that information I begged her to get a second opinion. This was a clear case of a doctor with the focus on one thing, money.

She tried to request her medical records back from the oncologist and refused and delayed. She ended up a week later in emergency room wherein a different doctor was able to evaluate her and confirmed she didn't have cancer. Her bladder didn't need to be removed. He performed a simple out-patient surgery, which was all she needed. This is mind blowing right? I am sure as you are reading this, you have a few stories of your own to share.

The pharmaceutical industry is like an iceberg. We only see what we want but are ignorant of the infrastructure and characteristics that make it what it are. These smaller examples of greed are the tip but the expansive iceberg reaches all the way to the global elites, who want to control de-populate the world to 500 million. Don't take my word for it, the World Health Organization isn't hiding their agenda. However, here in America, Big Pharma and our government have plenty to cover up.

Many people in developed nations like the United States have a hard time accessing alternative medicine. The healthcare industry is not exactly free of scandals and problems, but they are business entities. The goal is to make money, which often times is to our detriment.

The basis of pharmaceutical drugs is to keep us sick. As a business, their goal is to keep us in fear and keep us sick. Big Pharma is protecting their interests by not accepting the efficacy of alternative medicine. They know the harmful side effects of medications.

For mental illness, doctors tell you that you need to take it for life. Do they recommend exercise as a way to reduce anxiety and depression? Absolutely not! Everyone knows including doctors that we should first try what is natural before resorting to surgery and medication. But they are incentivized to push pharmaceutical drugs. Big Pharma pays doctors thousands of dollars to put as many people on medications as possible.

Our healthcare industry needs to allow people the information and option to try other healing alternatives. Even when cures for AIDS and CANCER have been discovered over 40 years ago by Dr. Royal Rife and others. Big Pharma and our government steps in to squash it, de-validate it and hide it from us.

In fact, when the Red Cross was publishing on YouTube that in 1 day children were no longer showing AIDS in Africa, America stepped in to claim it a hoax, as billions of dollars were at stake if they didn't get their medication to market.

Unfortunately, our doctors are only trained to prescribe medicines or perform surgeries. It's on purpose. It was designed that way. Many doctors cannot be blamed as they don't know the bigger, corrupt picture. But a growing number of medical professionals do get exposed to the corrupt greed that exists. This is especially true during and after the pandemic.

Unfortunately, it has become a venture where billions of dollars can be gained despite our need for healing. Many civilizations have used technologies and modalities that are far more effective and advanced than what is used in western medicine in the last century.

Furthermore, suppose the government and pharmaceutical industries are all about their interest. In that case, doctors should have the permission or right to tell patients about alternative medicines and cures for diseases and illnesses. They are pawns, controlled by the system.

Anybody who claimed to heal anyone outside the medical field is condemned, shunned, jailed, and oftentimes killed. Lookup people like Dr. Bruzinsky, Andreas Klaus, Nikola Tesla, and Dr. Rife.

I personally witnessed the disappearances of many successful healers. I know many healers who had their businesses shut down because they called their clients "patients" and used terms like "cured," "treated," or "diagnosed." Why is that so bad? Doctors "practice" medicine. Why can't we all be there for the common good to help people heal?

Providers of alternative medicine are not allowed to say those words. Those words are only allowed by a licensed medical professional. Even when countless people have been shown to overcome even the most deadly diseases through natural means, no hint of healing can be mentioned. It's ok for Big Pharma to advertise their prescription medications while hiding and/or minimizing the dangerous side effects they can have. Doesn't that seem ludicrous?

Yet, a naturopath cannot make any claim, regardless of the service or remedy, to successfully help or resolve someone's disease or illness, all without side effects, and not run into big trouble. It is heart- breaking that our healthcare system claims to be the best in the world. Still, it is merely a monopoly business that prevents us from getting to the root cause and getting people better forever.

So know you know why you don't know more about these alternative healing modalities. We are at risk for recommending, offering, and facilitating anything that is healing, that is not medical. Our healthcare system and Big Pharma do not make money by getting people well. So they will do anything and everything to prevent these hidden secrets from being revealed. Keep us sick, and continue to deceive us.

The goal to keep people sick, is disgusting, selfish, and greedy. In fact, it's pure evil. It's time we open our eyes and see things for how they really are. We now live in an age where we can get information globally. The answers are often right there in front of us, but did you know that these answers are often twisted to defer you or block you the next time you search for them?

With Google at our fingertips we could and should find answers to everything. Well, that is what you think, but not true. Much is hidden from you. If you are lucky enough to find something, the next time you search it, it will likely be gone. Access to successful healing methods are being banned, hidden and even fake media is pushed to our news channels and internet feeds with false information.

We are banned in a country that says we have freedom! Just like other third world countries are controlled from having access to Amazon, or on-line shopping, we are being controlled too. Freedom to choose, freedom to speak and freedom to live! Even our holistic wellness center has been banned from Facebook because we used the word "holistic." Anyone who shows success in healing, is a threat to Big Pharma and our gov-ernment.

Anytime we try to help people by offering natural solutions, we are banned from social media. People cannot find us or access our alternative healing methods if we are hidden from sight. Search engines like DuckDuckGo are best be-cause they do not filter out information like Google. Yes, this is true! Even your Facebook is designed to filter information and send you in the wrong direction for you to be misguided back to the corrupt ways of keeping us ill.

It was even released on Twitter, after Elon Musk took over, that the truth about the vaccinations and the harm they cause, where held from us. News channels, again, all being controlled by one entity, controls them on what to say and not say.

We can learn a lot from our ancestors in the art of healing. The pharmaceutical business is threatened by holistic and natural ways because they work. They are helping people heal and get better, but that is not how our health system is designed. Our pharmaceutical companies are monopolizing our health and our future. It is all about money and how to get the most and keep us sick for their benefit.

There are many good people out there trying to do their best to help people heal. Doctors are trained with limited solutions, prescribing medications and conducting surgeries. They are not taught about nutrition and are discouraged practice anything outside of the realm of prescribing medication and surgery. Habits like getting sunshine, laughing, eating healthy, practicing yoga or meditation, taking herbs, and homeopathic remedies are not considered.

Back 20 years ago, when I would see the doctor, they were not even open to these ideas, methods, and concepts. Today, those are more familiar and mainstream, so doctors are more accepting of them. Now, new technologies are slowly re-emerging (technologies that existed centuries ago) like infrared light therapy, biofeedback, neurofeedback, energy healing, frequency medicine, and quantum healing are being doubted and rejected by the medical community. If natural and holistic methods are compatible with the western theme (to heal), why else would they discourage and ban them?

The government should care more about its citizens. Alternative medicines can help build a vibrant and healthier society. But that won't give them power, control and billions of dollars.

If I was in a car accident or had a life-threatening infection, there is no doubt that I would want doctors to gather up my guts from the highway and sew me back up. Outside of that, everyone should be encouraged to try natural solutions over medications and surgery.

Why do we trust so much in medication and surgeries before we try natural alternatives? Little do you know, before pharmaceuticals our ancestors used ingredients such as herbs, essential oils, frequency medicine, energy healing, etc.! These natural remedies were highly effective before medications and vaccinations where introduced. Now causing an extreme rise in auto-immune diseases, cancers and autism.

Let's compare America with other countries and see how patients are treated first and foremost. Most governments of other countries pay for healthcare, which is equal for everyone. Therefore, there is no financial incentive behind it. It is not a money-making business. In America, doctors get incentivized, sometimes $500 to $1,500, for every medication they prescribe, by the pharmaceutical companies that manufacture them. They don't care whether you need it; it becomes a money motivator. In other countries, doctors are rewarded for getting their clients healthier by helping their patients loose weight, get off medications, quit smoking, and maintaining a healthier lifestyle.

Here in America, people are getting sicker every year. Diseases such as autoimmune and autism never existed 10-20 years ago. Every medical professional who prescribes medicines knows that with each medication, there are side effects, and with those side effects, more treatments are prescribed. This creates a toxic profile in the person that spirals them into more and more symptoms, weakening their immune system.

Please don't take my word for it; research and learn about these facts yourself. We are not shown the truth or given the truth. People who speak the truth are often muted, punished or even killed so you have to look on places that are not controlled such as TruthSocial, Telegram, Childers Health Defense, Joe Rogan, Rumble, or The Epoch Times. Even Elon Musk had to buy Twitter so freedom of speech could be heard again. Whitney Webb is another brave soul who is exposing the truths. Look her up too.

We need to turn things around, open our eyes and speak up to make change. I look forward to the day when western medicine doctors incorporate holistic and natural methods offered as a first resort. I have helped thousands of clients globally. These clients prayed and searched and found me through word of mouth. I have people come to me from all over the world, having tried everything, including surgeries and medications. They, "my clients", are usually at the end of their rope, sometimes in their final hour, desperate and hopeless. (Remember, I cannot say "patients" because, again, the medical community owns that word, and I would get in trouble for it or even be put out of business.)

The good news is that when someone comes to me at this desperate stage, they are open to anything. Sadly, they get to this point before they are willing to accept trying something new and opening their minds to something different. Again, these technologies and modalities that I speak of are not new. They have existed for centuries. Frequency medicine, invented by doctor Royal Rife in the 1900s, was claimed to cure AIDS and cancer. Anyone remotely affiliated with him was sent to prison. Many of the technologies are not allowed or prohibited in the United States.

Fortunately, his technology has continued to live on, (underground and in secret), helping thousands of people. These technologies are kept hidden and secret to help people heal. I have personally witnessed only positive outcomes from such devices. After all, we are all energy, and when you use energy to change energy, you switch from outside-in healing (medications) to inside-out healing. This is the most effective form of healing that I know of. Many great people in our past tried to make a difference and still do.

Nikola Tesla, for instance, was not even mentioned in our history books in school. He created and gave free energy to the world; with his ideas, technology was destroyed, and so was he.

Keep us dumb, weak, and distracted so that we become sheep while greed and corruption destroy humanity. Truth and the healing of light and love will prevail. The truth about advanced technology and natural healing will become more known and available.

"Foolish the doctor who despises the knowledge acquired by the ancients."

— HIPPOCRATES

4
INSURANCE COVERAGE

"Health insurance should be a given for every citizen."

— JESSE VENTURA

My intention is not to condemn western medicine but rattle the foundation on which healthcare is based in the US. For most Americans, it is viewed as the only effective, available option for healthcare. That is what we are force-fed to believe through TV and other media. There are many scenarios where medical intervention will save your life.

The best western medicine is only available to those who can afford a premium insurance policy, such as a PPO.

There is no ethical explanation for why only the very rich deserve optimal health care and why advanced technologies and remedies are not allowed in the US. Our government has yet to be able to implement a healthcare solution that offers equal access to apex healthcare services for everyone.

This again means that its citizens rely on people who provide healthcare insurance coverage to families, individuals, or their dependents. Furthermore, insurance is a government-run program that attempts to cover the healthcare expenses of specific groups in society. If you are conversant with the system, you will notice that there are different types, and people can choose according to some factors, including income.

Getting health insurance coverage in the US is as complex as the system itself, and if you think your wealth will deliver access on a platter of gold, then you are in for a wild ride. One must be fully aware of the features of each type when picking the right insurance coverage.

Now for another story on this topic, I was called to fly to meet a client who has a stroke and was placed in a nursing home. When I saw her she was drugged up (sedated) and told she was a vegetable. The nursing home would be collecting thousands of dollars for years to come, easy 15 years in my estimation.

The family's goal was to see if we could get her to a point where she could use the restroom on her own. This was the only way they would be comfortable taking her home. The husband and son were her only support. Upon my arrival, I requested to see a list of all medications the client was on. I then requested that all sedatives and medications be removed. In my research 3 medications were found to be fatal if taken together! I quickly gained the confidence in my clients after that discovery. If you are taking care of a loved one, you better research each medication and understand their side effects and even reactions to each other. Many times by simply removing the medications, the client will get better.

The doctors immediately removed the medications, wherein the nursing home put up a fight to stop her sedatives. They were not happy with me at all. I was on to them. I was a threat to their business, but what about the quality of life for this woman? What about the other 100 people stuck in there all sedated as well? It was really sad and scary.

Finally, with all things removed I began my work. I hung a sign on her door to not come in. She was super weak, and instead of getting 4 nurses to assist her to the bathroom, it was going to me, the husband and son. She happened to have a urinary tract infection so her need to go was frequent. I used this to our advantage. I performed brain optimization in between helping her first stand and timing it each time, we saw progress and strength quickly restore in her legs. Before the day was over she was standing on her own. The next day we practiced standing on one leg so that when she started to walk she would have the strength. Before you knew it, and within the 4 days I had with her, she was able to remember how to get up, and go to the bathroom on her own. According to the family, she was ready to go home!

There were a few things we needed to work out. The family wanted her to get support for her rehabilitation, now that she has progressed so far. However, her insurance refused any more treatments to help her further. They literally denied her of any services related to that, even when told of her amazing progress. Medicare basically wrote her off after the stroke, and gave her 10 days recover and since it was beyond that time, she had no additional support to further her progress.

My time was up. I didn't want to go without offering some sort of help. So I contacted an in-home nurse that could further support her for 30 days while she could continue to get stronger and stronger. Fear began to set in with the husband, worrying about what if she fell or couldn't go to the restroom at night. The second issue was the nursing home drug their feet to "discharge her". They insisted the family wait for the newly hired director.

The nursing home began to put her right back on the meds and sedatives and she was on prior to my visit. She was now stuck there once again. The family felt they had no choice but to give into the corrupt system. The family didn't have the means to provide her the continued support. The system failed her as it does thousands of others.

I am sadly witness to it time and time again. I have seen hundreds of my clients told they would not live or walk or function. In 1-2 weeks, with my services, they have their life back. But they are up against a system that wants the financial gain over the person's well-being.

Now in contrast, I was hired to work on another stroke client, located in Denver. He had optimal PPO insurance. He was given ample recovery time with no limit on his treatments for brain optimization. He has recovered 100% after being locked in paralysis for 4 months and needed to relearn how to eat, walk, talk, etc. Both clients had equally severe strokes. I provided them the same protocol, but the care they received from the medical system was vastly different. It was all because of their insurance coverage. One died, and one lived.

Many people feel not only is the healthcare system corrupt, so are insurance companies. They collect thousands of dollars and we cannot even get the care we need.

Lack of Price Transparency

Fraud and cover-up are familiar stories in the corridors of the US healthcare system. Whether from the government, healthcare officials, or doctors and nurses, it is rampant and not good. At this junction, transparency between policy-holders/makers, providers, and insurance providers is the norm. The healthcare insurance buyers (you and I) want more from the insurance providers, but all we see are premium charges to employers and low payouts. This leaves consumers with no pathway to control their decisions about their health, cost, or results.

Challenges in Finding a Good Doctor

Most consumers rely on online information on medical sites when accessing or finding a good doctor or facility for their treatment. This is impeded by inaccessibility to adequate information that properly informs the patient about their next move. Consumers are faced with indecision: finding the doctor with the right skill to treat a condition, accessing wait times, staff friendliness, and more. While I will not compare accessibility with alternative treatments, it offers consumers a better offer from the practitioner and even the opportunity to ask questions before making a choice.

. . .

QUALITY OF CARE

The US spends hugely on healthcare, and one would think that the results are outstanding, but they differ from other developed countries like the Nether- lands, Sweden, Canada, and even Switzerland. In fact, while the US actually performed exceptionally on consumer needs, it scored less on other health metrics, including quality care, infant mortality, safe care, and unmanaged diabetes.

Healthcare Cost in America

According to a 2020 report, US healthcare spending per person averages over $12,500, the highest in the world. While the high-cost cuts across all the care sectors, the reasons are not far-fetched.

The Need for New Technology

We are in the digital age, yet many healthcare centers and facilities operate manually. There is an immense need to incorporate technology to simplify the process, and it is expensive. Today, technology plays a crucial part in understanding, appreciating, and implementing medical strategies and alternatives that cater to everyone, regardless of their status or coverage. As the system modernizes and integrates medical technologies like artificial intelligence, the Internet of Things, and remote monitoring, healthcare professionals have stream- lined workflow and created efficient approaches that communicate with patients better. This entire enhancement is paid for by the services rendered. The pandemic showed how unprepared the global healthcare system was, but even more how it shattered the health infrastructure developed nations thought could cater to emergencies like COVID-19. Since the pandemic, the healthcare system has worked hard to optimize, prioritize, and implement operable amenities to curb its excesses or bridge missed loopholes.

Too Many Uninsured Americans

There are about 26 million uninsured Americans, and probably many have never bought health insurance coverage ever. This causes many to face undue health hardship or stay away from hospitals due to the high cost. However, since the Affordable Care Act was signed into law, many Americans have had access to medicine and doctors. It has also reduced the discrimination encountered by many in the healthcare sector.

Furthermore, children, young adults, and seniors have better health coverage and access to subsidized prescription drugs.

Inefficiencies in the Healthcare Sector

Medical Care Workers' Shortage

The shortage of workers in the US was exposed by the pandemic. The problem is significant and challenging but must be combated now. A staff shortage in the healthcare sector is choking the system, according to a 2021 report by industry market analysis firm Mercer. The report states that by 2025, the shortage will extend to all sectors, including home health aides, nursing assistants, lab technicians, nurse practitioners, and others.

Another study published by the AAMC predicts a shortage of 54,100 and 139,000 primary and specialty care physicians by 2033. While many say hiring more care workers will solve the problem, it is not straightforward as the following issues continue to linger in the healthcare sector.

Lack of Insurance Coverage

We cannot emphasize this fact enough. When many people are uninsured, it gives the wrong impression that the sector has enough. Still, as many people get insurance coverage, we realize the healthcare sector needs more hands to cover everyone. Furthermore, there is uneven care across different levels caused by the type of health insurance coverage. That means consumers receive varying levels of care by location or plan; patients in rural areas have less access to physicians, while those in urban regions get more than they need.

Let's have a brief insight into alternative medicine. Alternative medicine is any medical practice that is unproven and not considered part of mainstream medicine due to the lack of facts supporting its effectiveness. Over the years, alternative medicine has become popular, but most Americans do not understand this treatment.

Although alternative medicine has not received the recognition it deserves, many trust it because they have tried it when western medicine has failed them.

If you are insured and want to opt for alternative medicine for your ailment, be sure to get a PPO with out-of-network coverage. Medicaid and

Medicare do not typically cover alternative treatments.

The benefits of alternative treatment are not considered, but rather disregarded entirely. The purpose of this book is to open your eyes to the possibilities that exist outside of conventional treatment options. Alternative treatment can reverse all diseases, whether minor or death-threatening, including terminal illnesses.

Many have benefitted from these treatments, but do not take our word for it, but as Mark Twain says, "Be careful about reading health books. You may die of a misprint."

There is still more to do to bring the healthcare sector to an efficient, affordable, and accessible standard for every citizen. We have hope for a future that consists of healthy and strong citizens.

5
A LITTLE ABOUT ME

I was born with a heightened awareness of the energy around me. As a toddler, I already understood that everything was made up of energy. I was meditating by age 6 and working with the flow of energy before I understood what I was doing. We lived in a small farming town in the Midwest. When work on the farm would suddenly halt because our tractor broke down, we lacked money and food. I would offer to go with my father into the field so I could turn the tractor back on for him, using my energy.

I didn't understand how I knew what to do, only that I would make a "connection" with the energy around me and channel it into the broken tractor using my mind, intention, and energy.

Although we never really talked about it, my father recognized my luck to somehow "fix" farm equipment so that he could be back up and running. I didn't tell people about my ability to manifest positive outcomes using energy because I knew narrow-minded folks in town would judge and ridicule me. I started experimenting with my abilities more and more often, relying solely on my intuition for guidance.

I wasn't shy, but I didn't crave the limelight and wasn't interested in using my gifts for my own benefit. I used it to help others in need whenever I could by shifting the energy around them to create more positive outcomes. I remember when I got old enough to watch movies and saw the movie Carrie. It was based on a novel of the same name by Stephen King. If you're unfamiliar with this cult classic, it is about an abused teen named Carrie who uses her supernatural powers to get revenge. I remember feeling like I understood Carrie's powers, except that my ability worked oppositely—turning negatives into positives.

When I was about ten, I learned that my cousin was dying of thyroid disease, and he had bulging eyeballs and was really skinny. My aunt became frustrated with the doctors because they could not help him and informed my aunt (his mom) that he would die. My aunt took matters into her own hands. Rather than accepting this diagnosis, she used natural remedies to completely heal him. She became incredibly knowledgeable about herbs and essential oils in a short amount of time. She was not about to give up hope for her son's recovery.

Doctors were amazed at my cousin's recovery, but rather than recognizing what my aunt had done, they called it a miracle. Years later, when my grand- mother was 73 and dying of leukemia, my aunt also used herbs and essential oils to pro- long her life. My grandmother recovered from her cancer, and again the doctors were amazed. But similar to the last time, they did not believe my aunt's ministrations had anything to do with it. My grandmother went on to live until she was ninety-five, and in the years after she recovered from cancer, she was very healthy and active. I was lucky to learn about herbal medicine and the healing properties of various oils from my aunt.

This was the Eureka moment when I realized it was possible to heal diseases naturally.

I knew I was only scratching the surface of my own potential, and I became increasingly eager to learn more. I was a big fish in a little pond, and as I got older, I began to dream about moving to a big city and finding out what else I could do with my gifts. I headed to New York City (NYC). I joined an elite group of people who studied meditation, martial arts, and computer programming. I remember being immediately intrigued by the prospect.

As it turns out, joining that group was one of the best things I ever did. It was the first time I learned to meditate. The other group members and I learned to put a protective energetic bubble around ourselves. Apparently, I'd been meditating without knowing I was doing it since I was a child. We practiced walking around in our bubbles to see if we could avoid being noticed. I learned about the meta- physical body and how to work more deeply with energy, using it as a powerful tool for manifesting positive things in my personal life.

The group was led by an enlightened Buddhist Master that believed that computer programming was good for the brain and concentration, as was martial arts, with the added benefit of strengthening the physical body. Both disciplines were beneficial for increasing our facility to reach an enhanced meditative state. Membership fees for the group were expensive. It was $5,000 per month, and being a student, I had to work five jobs to afford it. I began teaching meditation to all the Ivy League schools for free. It was mindblowing to hear from students, how my meditation classes helped them recover from depression, suicide, anxiety, and more.

We were taught how to maximize our earning potential, and at eighteen years old, I was already making $100 per hour doing computer programming. The other people in the group were all multi-millionaires, something I would eventually become myself. I learned to appreciate the security afforded by financial freedom, which contributed to my own financial success. I was still only eighteen and in the early stages of my career. Because I had just started dating again, I decided to get a pap smear. I didn't hear anything back after the test, so I assumed everything was fine. I spent the next two years building several companies in the healthcare field.

I have always been empathetic towards people who suffer from pain regardless of emotional, mental, physical or spiritual imbalance. One late night, I tried to help my first of many victims. I was walking home from my waitress job after volunteering to wash all the dishes on Christmas Eve. El Toritos Restaurant was located in the Empire State Building and we had a full house that day. I needed extra money, so did anything and everything extra to make ends meet. It was about 3AM, I was exhausted but decided to walk home because it began to snow. Not a car was around, it was so quiet that you could hear the large lumps of snow falling to the ground. Nearly home to my high-rise apartment, I passed a young man, sitting on the side of the Grand Central Station building. He was nearly covered in snow. He looked nearly frozen. There wasn't a soul on the streets at that time except him. I offered for him to come to my place to sleep, get warm and eat before he left the next morning. I was so tired, but literally stayed up the entire night waiting for the clock to turn 7am so I could send him on his way. I was terrified but determined to help. He was eternally grateful and I don't regret doing that, however I was fortunate to not get hurt in the process.

***

Now, fast forwarded to when I was twenty, I received a letter in the mail informing me that the Pap smear I had two years prior shows I had stage 4 cancer! To say I was shocked would be a terrible understatement. The letter said I didn't need to make an appointment but should come to the hospital to be seen as soon as possible. I remember seeing a payphone about 20 feet away and felt like the bionic woman, walking in slow motion towards the phone to call my mom. She was always supportive and encouraged me to go right away to the hospital.

When I arrived at the hospital, I noticed several other young women standing around looking the way I felt, all clutching letters in their hands. It appeared the hospital had lost several patients' records and only recently found them. At the hospital, they put me through plenty of tests to confirm the authenticity of the test results. When the results came back, I was given a clean bill of health. To this day, I do not know whether I healed myself by raising my own energetic vibration or if it was a hospital error. Instead of getting angry or suing the hospital for their mistake, I developed software for women to track abnormal pap smears.

The software meant women would be guaranteed a follow-up with their results. I sold the company and rebranded and expanded it towards women receiving pap smears, colonoscopies and mammograms. I sold that as well. That version was used globally by the Department of Defense. After the events of 9/11, any non-military vendor was shut out.

I loved living in the big city, and Chicago was more affordable than NYC. I wasn't only focused on entrepreneurial endeavors while I was in Chicago. During that time, I also got married and had two children. Nine years later, I ended up moving back to NYC with my children after losing my husband.

While there, I built another company which also became very successful. I created one of the first e-health records, blossoming and worth $20 million. I was a pioneer, and my work caught the attention of big players like General Electric,

Microsoft, Northrop Grumman, Google, and Accenture. It was a thrilling time in my life, but being an entrepreneur is never without its challenges.

After publicly sharing what I had created, the government began to offer the same thing for free; this essentially put me out of business. To top it off, the financial market crashed in 2008, and I lost all my investors. I kept the business running from my personal savings for two more years paying seven executives top salaries. I tried selling what we had. Several years later, after the death of a CTO from a competitor, developers admitted a company in California stole my source code therefore didn't make the purchase of my company. All those factors were hard to bare. But being able to move on after a business failure is a sign of being a good entrepreneur.

I was not having fun anymore, so I took what I had learned and moved to the West coast with my children. While there, I founded a couple other companies. They were on my bucket list. The small town I had moved to had very little culture, so I decided to open an art gallery. Every month was like a party, with a theme and tying in ways to raise money for the Red Cross during Hurricane Katrina, The Kidney Foundation and more. All the while I continued to see people one-on-one for their health needs. That lasted about two years then I founded an organic salsa company, which became national in less than a year. But my passion continued to focus on health beyond food.

So I founded my holistic wellness center. Initially, it was just me, and then I grew it to help more people. The goal was to help people heal themselves from a broad range of health conditions in a natural and non-invasive way, without using medications or surgery. Having passionate, caring providers trained in the technology and methodologies I vetted made it a success.

I was able to offer new quantum healing technologies where we can help facilitate healing regardless of where they are in the world. I led with brain optimization, which promotes healing by bringing balance to the brain. When the brain is in balance, symptoms go away, and so does the label. I introduced several other innovative and highly effective healing therapies, including light therapy, frequency healing, bio-scanning, and many more.

It wasn't long after launching my wellness center, the success stories started pouring in. Word spread, and soon we could not keep up with the demand from clients without expanding to other parts of the world.

I am not a doctor, nor do I have a medical degree. I am however certified and licensed in all the technology and modalities we provide. Many of these are not even known in America. We do not diagnose, but rather our modalities can detect. We do not cure, but rather we facilitate our clients own ability to heal themselves.

With 25+ years of real life experiences, witnessing clients miracles through natural means, is valuable. Sharing factual information from personal experience along with highly advanced technologies, hopefully opens your eyes, your heart and your mind to hearing new possibilities.

My time here on this earth is fully directed in helping people heal. I am so grateful for the teachers, scientists, doctors, coroners, researchers who guided me along the way. It is my contribution to share my experiences and truths for healing with you. There is no reason, whatsoever;

you can't have optimal health too. Focus on that which you want.

As stories of people "miraculously" healing themselves poured in, I realized I needed to make these services available to everyone. I turned the center into a not-for-profit organization because the services were cost-prohibitive for many would-be clients. It was important to me that cost or insurance status is not the deciding factor for whether a person can get help to heal themselves.

I am truly blessed to have never worked a day in my life. I found my purpose and my path, to help stop the suffering of humankind.

6

UNDERSTANDING THE ROOT CAUSE

"For every effect there is a root cause. Find & address the root cause rather than try to fix the effect, as there is no end to the latter."

— CELESTINE CHUA

*O*utside an accident, like falling out of a tree or crashing your car, the root causes are commonly derived from some prior trauma such as the death of a loved one, or abusive relationship.

Isn't it common to ignore a problem until it becomes a problem? Being diagnosed with any disease or having an ailment reoccur without knowing why is overwhelming. It is only fair to find the root cause, whether it is cancer or an allergy. Most times, when we get an adverse doctor's report, we start to process our death and how detrimental it can get. Well, if you are the one that prefers to ignore a situation rather than tackle it head-on, read this chapter carefully.

When we get bad news about our health, do not fear it. Ask yourself the following questions:

- Why do I have this disease?
- What is causing the disease?
- Am I contributing to my condition?
- Am I preventing my body from healing itself?
- What is the best healing approach for this illness?

Most of the time, all we do is to add to our problems; they only worsen the situation. Medication is a Band-Aid that causes increased side effects. Surgery can also be a Band-Aid such as in cancer. Many of my clients have their breasts or colon removed and their cancer comes back. Do you wonder why? Did we address the root cause? In my experience, without addressing the root cause, we only delay a bigger problem down the road. I have had countless clients try medication after medication and surgery after surgery, only to find themselves in a much worse situation.

So, where do we begin? Largely a physical issue stems from your mental and emotional health! However, let us understand that the universe is an energy-filled system. Next is to believe that our bodies attract what we give out. This book emphasizes the fact that energies and vibrations surround us. Humans are energy, and when our vibrational frequency is off-balanced, it reflects on our physical selves as pain or illnesses emanating from our thoughts (mental) or emotions. When we understand and accept this fact, it is easy to understand and want to know the underlying cause of disease and believe we can heal ourselves.

It feels hard to grasp, but it is the truth. In the previous chapter, we discussed the consequence of fear on our minds and body and the resultant effect. We talked about how fear triggers the body to release chemicals like cortisol, which makes the brain act otherwise. However, when these chemicals flood our system, even though it is for a good cause, the suddenness is detrimental to our bodies. The result is a heart-related disease and others. To heal, we must go to the source. And we begin with how we perceive or feel illnesses today.

Do you know that how you perceive an illness can boost self-healing capabilities? Imagine this: you go for a test, and the result shows you have a blockage somewhere that is causing the constant headaches you bothering you.

You might genuinely have a bad result, but if you think positive thoughts about healing and do not allow the report to trigger fear, you might/will overcome the disease faster than individuals who take the negative route.

So, do you see how your mental understanding played a role? However, the root cause of a disease is not when the doctor or yourself discovered it. It is not the anxiety or fear that causes it but the conditions, lifestyle, and past experiences that we are engaged in or have previously. For every action, there is a reaction. Health is accumulating many wrong things or ignoring too many right things.

Unresolved issues over a long time frame can magnify the root cause of any disease. When we understand this, we can look for a solution. Furthermore, how does emotion play into this? How you feel honestly about an ailment divulges a lot.

When you get the doctor's report, what did you do? How does the condition make you feel? Are you partly responsible for it? Remember, the ailment is not why you act the way you do because you ignored it for a long time. It is just the manifestation of everything that has happened.

Every health condition begins as a mental and emotional root before a physical manifestation. If you believe there is more to a health issue, you will receive more because that is the frequency you emit in nature and what you receive.

It is hard to believe, but trust me, everything around you works on the energy frequency you absorb. Our bodies react based on the mental and emotional energy we give, and until we come to terms with this fact, we will recycle patterns and drown in unresolved pain and trauma to our detriment. With that said, science says there are five root causes of a disease or the current state of your health.

. . .

Pathogens & Toxins

Outside of trauma induced illnesses, are those that are pathogenic. Most diseases and illnesses reside in the body, in the gut. What do I mean by pathogenic? Pathogens consist of viruses, bacteria, fungus, para- sites, EMFs, and heavy metals. Our bodies are filled with these things, especially as we age, travel, things we eat like fish, pork, or other types of meat. Even on vegetables, parasites can transfer into our bodies. Oh, and of course, our beloved pets as we kiss them after they have licked their bum.

Most people are shocked to hear that they have parasites, but we all carry them to some degree. Where it becomes a concern is when it weakens our immune system. When our immune system weakens, we can no longer detox and fight off infections and other illnesses. As we get older, the harder it gets. However, there are many causative agents for diseases, and if you take the guesswork out, these might just be it.

They are chemicals in our food, environment, and drinks that cause health problems or exasperate the risk of getting a disease. Although the connection between toxins and disease is mysterious, you know better. Toxins impact every aspect of our lives, including our mental health, causing depression, anxiety, autoimmune disease, cancer, and even death. They are in our food, including alcohol, preservatives, sugar, and cigarettes. But how do toxins cause illness?

They upset the balance of the body when it is weak, leading to health issues and even cancer. A common thread in cancers is when parasites multiply in the body because of too much Candida. Candida occurs when there is too much sugar in the body. The parasites burrow into the walls of your organs to create tumors.

By killing the Candida, its food, and the parasites, the tumors begin to heal on their own. But when we do not know about these things, they become infected and thus turn into cancers. Cutting out parts of our bodies that have cancer may spare us some time, but it does not get to the root cause. Until we kill the pathogens, cancer will return.

Additionally, using radiation and chemotherapy to kill cancer is not the right approach. We should not kill to heal but heal to heal. Stress is the number one cause of disease and illness. Therefore, we must look at emotions. Things that are stressful or traumatic in our lives and, if not dealt with properly, show up later as a disease in the body. Think of the word "disease."

Drinking tap water will cause an iodine deficiency in your body because of the fluoride in the water. Continuously drinking fluoridated water will lead to a toxic goiter or thyroidism. If toxins are not the root causes of a disease, what is it?

Trauma

With every client, I can usually trace them back to a brutal or tragic event in their life, and at the end of the day; they realize that unresolved past emotions led them down the path to physical ailments.

Diseases will leverage our inability to let go or deal with a terrible past to invade our lives. Trauma is one of the root causes of ailments and illnesses in our lives. Therefore, it is paramount to understand how this 6-letter word possesses so much power to affect our mental, emotional, and physical selves.

Trauma is any unpleasant circumstance or experience that happens in our life that is distressing to us. For example, a child that witnesses a war or a victim of rape can live in so much fear that it is detrimental to their health. Many traumatic events stem from childhood, but traumatic events can happen at any time.

Trauma can trigger toxin build-up, deficiencies, infection, and lifestyle changes, but why trauma does have a tremendous effect on our health is fantastic. People who have experienced trauma have the protective hormones cortisol and adrenaline that trigger the freeze, fight, or flight reaction. Usually, with help, it is easy to restore how these hormones flood into the body system. When trauma is left untreated and unresolved, the experiences that caused the trauma can continuously cause a release any time the victim recalls, sees, or hears situations resembling the incident.

People deal with trauma by eating unhealthy and indulging in nasty habits like smoking, drinking, substance abuse, and unprotected sexual activity. While these are coping mechanisms, they contribute to chronic diseases like cancer, heart-related conditions, mental and emotional problems, and social isolation. The fundamental problem is that people who have suffered a traumatic event are subconsciously unaware of how their system reacts to the thought of it. It is not a conscious choice to trigger the coping mechanism, but the underlying cause will continue to lower our energy frequency and make us prone to diseases until we deal with it.

Dealing with the Root Cause

A healthy body is a powerful tool capable of finding and healing any condition, including determining the root cause. We live in an energy-surrounding universe that sends out vibrations according to the vibrations we send out. Creating a balanced energy level with the earth or nature will help curb many of the problems we suffer from today. Our society heavily depends on medications, surgeries, and pharmaceuticals as the only healing option. Instead, when we know the root cause in the first place, we will enjoy other curative and preventive options to ensure we never suffer again.

The power to heal is within you. Understanding how to control this energy and use it gives you immense power. Look at it this way; when we are healthy, the energy level is at 100%, but situations like fear, trauma, infection, unhealthy lifestyle, or use the same energy to enhance their effect. At this point, the positive energy is minimal, while the negative energy takes precedence. However, when you remember you are in control, it is easy to switch all negative thoughts and events with positive energy that reverses illnesses and chronic conditions that weakens us.

I write to you with hardships of my own. From stage 4 cancer, to being raped and having had an abortion, being kidnapped and escaping, losing 2 babies to miscarriage, losing 2 husbands, 2 years extreme physical and mental abuse, losing a multi-million dollar company I built to a larger company who stole, monopolized out of greed and power, being a single mom and raising 2 kids with zero child support, losing my mother to cancer before I knew what I know now, and nearly losing my own grown child to the vaccination.

Seeing these life events listed is nearly unbelievable, to even me! I also know there are others out there who experienced worse. But each time I had experienced extreme pain or trauma, I refused to let it effect me. I chose not to carry it forward or re-live it.I am grateful for each of these experience and life lessons for it has made me who I am today. I chose not to be a victim, I chose not to live in my past and I chose to not let it effect me negatively or I knew I would be very sick. I chose not to sue countless. What doesn't kill you makes you stronger.

Please stop suffering in your pain, and if you are reading this chapter, this is a call that there are alter- native ways to curb even what the world terms a terminal disease. Many people use the power of the energy within to heal themselves.

"The body is a self-healing organism, so it is about clearing the way so the body can heal itself." insurance should be a given for every citizen."

— BARBARA BRENNAN

7
GATHERING THE FACTS &
WEIGHING THE OPTIONS

"Knowing when you should weigh up your options, remain calm and not take everything at face value has certain benefits. Ending the day with a peaceful soul is one".

— VIRGINIA ALISON

The whole point of writing this book is to bring awareness to you and to the world about the success of holistic and natural methods. So many truthful, factual, and scientifically proven methods have been shunned, mocked, banned, and hidden so that you stay sick and the pharmaceutical industry can thrive.

Some know that medication and surgery were not the only answers. Just because a doctor has prescribed medication does not mean you have to take it. It's time to open your mind and awareness to alternative medicine. I remember it was just two years ago when it was on the front cover of Time Magazine and National Geographic stating that alternative medicine is the new norm.

How accurate are the benefits and risks of a treatment your physician prescribes when you are sick? How much do you truly know about it?

I had to ask these questions because we blindly trust our healthcare system and are "brain-washed" that we cannot do anything alone. A couple of years ago, I came across this article from a systematic review of 48 studies stating that clinicians "rarely" had accurate expectations about the risks or benefits of a treatment. Sometimes it is underestimated or overestimated at your own risk.

***

A client of mine came to me because she was told she had bladder cancer. The doctor said he would have to remove her bladder and she would for-ever have to be inconvenienced with a bag to drain her urine. I ran my scan, found no cancer, just a benign cyst blocking the area to urinate. Furious of this doctors greedy plan, which was without merit, I told her my findings and begged her to get a second opinion. She took my advice, but her oncologist refused to give back her medical records, calling her a fool for risking her life. It went on like this for weeks.

Finally, she ended up having so much pain she went into the emergency room and they did their discovery. The second doctor confirmed there was no cancer and simply removed her cysts, quick and easy. Thank God she was ok and thank God she didn't blindly follow the first doctor.

Another client of mine had a rapid tumor forming under her arm. It was a non-cancerous but growing a mass. She ended up getting surgery and immediately the tumors spread. The more the biopsies, the more tumors appeared. Why is this? Imagine poking a b-hive. The bees quickly get angry and end up spreading everywhere. Well the tumor contains a nest of parasites, if you disturb the nest, it spreads. If you cut it out, you still didn't address the parasites.

This is your body and your health, so you must know more and question everything. When we start discussing treatment options for a condition or lingering ailment, remember this:

- Know all the facts about the condition.
- Know all the treatments available to cure or curb that condition.
- Understand the details and requirements of each treatment option.
- Understand the information you are reading (essential).
- Find a specialist, doctor or health practitioner who advocates for what YOU want.
- Follow your heart and gut and stick to the plan

You must understand this; your life depends on it. So when your doctor prescribes chemo-therapy, ask all the questions and follow up with research immediately. You will see negative re-marks before positive ones, so never deal with a disease from an emotional point of view. That is why many people get it wrong and why pharma-ceutical companies easily rope us in with their ideas. At some point, you should seek the advice of a professional or expect them to learn more about the treatment option(s) you have chosen to understand how applicable it is to your condition entirely. If your choices are different, talk to your doctor or get a referral to a professional in that field that has used the said treatment option with high benefits. If you opt for natural, holistic, or alternative medicine, find experts in that field while you know about your options. While you wait for more details from the experts, talk to people and be positive throughout the journey.

One piece of advice I will give at this point is to connect with spirit and listen to your inner voice. Listen to your heart and what feels right for you. While you go on a soul-searching journey, have the following questions in mind:

- What don't I know that I don't know?
- What are my options beyond medication, chemotherapy or surgery?
- What have others done to successfully overcome this condition?
- How many others have successfully overcome this condition?
- How successful has your doctor or provider been?

- What did others do or not do?
- What more can be done?

When you have received answers to your questions, it is time to learn about your options. Always get a second opinion, whether with alternative treatments or modern medicine. Remember to voice your concerns about the treatment options. For example, does a treatment option go against your spiritual belief, diet, or culture? These concerns are essential, or you risk failing to finish the treatment option. Make sure you set yourself up for success. Be realistic with your financial ability to continue treatments, insurance support or not able to travel for your therapy, or follow the recommended protocol then you need to reconsider a path you can follow.

***

Another client of mine who came to me following a bilateral mastectomy due to cancer in the breast. Just as soon as the stitches healed the tumors burst out of her chest like molting lava. I was mortified having never seen such a sight. I ran a scan for a baseline, put her on a protocol that she followed to a tee. It was about 2 months before we fully got it under control to the point her cancer was not showing up any more. This was verified by her doctors. We were on the road to success.

Well, until suddenly her fears from others began to effect her that she wasn't doing enough, even though the cancer was now gone. She sought out another doctor, who basically told her that she would soon die, and he could slow it down but she needs to find the money to pay him for the rest of her life. I know this because I literally went with her to her appointment. He was rude and down right mean to her. I supported whatever she wanted to do. And with that, she proceeded to go down that path and ran out of money and her cancer tumors returned yet again. She regretted not sticking to our protocol and began to follow it once again, having realized she waisted energy, time and money.

This whole time she also was aware from our bio-scan, that her house was full of mold and radiation. She never moved or did anything about it. She died. There is no judgement. However, there is so much to learn from here.

· · ·

LET'S TAKE A LOOK:

- She was heavily influenced by the limiting beliefs and of western medicine
- She was negatively influenced by the fear of family and friends
- She did find an alternative that worked
- She didn't stick to what worked for her
- She didn't stay on the path that her heart led her to, but fell into the opinions of others
- She didn't set boundaries and surround herself with only those who supported her decisions
- She didn't address outside factors (the mold and radiation)

Do Your Own Research (DYOR)

Whether you are working with a team of experts or not, conduct your research, and believe me, the information is invaluable, and the sources are endless. However, beware of "fake" reports out there; they only trap the gullible ones among us. So please pay attention to who is giving the information and how many facts it contains.

- Remember these points as you seek answers.
- Journal your doubts, questions, and fears about the conditions and the treatments before you.
- Only seek information from credible, honest, and truthful people.
- Eliminate emotions; they get in the way of seeking truthful answers about your condition.
- Do not search alone; have a close friend or family member with you as you see the answers?
- Do not negate an option because it does not suit you or you dislike it; understand it first before you strike it out.

When you have your viable treatment options, what next? It is when you make a treatment decision by streamlining the accepted options until they boil down to just one. Whether it is modern or alternative medicine, you must ensure you are fully aware and ready to run with it.

Listen to this touching story on suppressing a cure for cancer, more than 40 years! **BURZYN-SKI: THE CANCER CURE COVER-UP - FULL**

DOCUMENTARY. The Cancer Cure Cover-up is the story of a pioneering biochemist who discovered a unique and proprietary method of successfully treating most cancers.

https://www.youtube.com/watch?v= rmxUsAI29fw

There is always a need for support on your journey. So share your decision with your family and friends or with your doctor or healer. Educate them as they need to know why you opted for that treatment; this is the best time to set the facts and reasons before them.

Sharyl Attkisson, discusses Astroturf, how information is distorted to the public. Tedx talk Feb. 2015.

You will encounter objections and problems with your choice, but you must be ready to go through it. Those who are not behind you, you should let them know that if they cannot support your decision and offer positive energy for your decision, they will have to be excluded until such time you are fully healed.

It is okay if you are unsure if you want any treatment for the condition. If you understand the risk and benefits involved and are willing to walk the 9 yards, which is great. I have seen cases where people are so overwhelmed with the treatment options and the processes that they opt out. While this is always a choice, make sure you understand why and that it is not emotionally inclined. If the decision is due to doubtful answers, search some more. If you are on this fact-finding journey for a loved one that has refused treatment, try talking to them about why the option is best and how delaying treatment is detrimental to their well-being. It may be the case but riddled with many obstacles.

Providers of holistic and natural medicine are still very much shut down and prevented from being able to make these fascinating technologies and remedies known again. Doctors often fear what they do not know or are not educated on, and many fear that if they inform patients of this option, they will lose out on the financial gain or put their practice at risk. Therefore, they often discourage and decline holistic and natural services for their patients. It doesn't matter if the patient gets well as long as they get paid. Insurance does not always cover alternative medicine, so many patients are skeptical about choosing natural and holistic measures as a treatment option for themselves.

Social media bans any mention of holistic and natural alternatives, and people who claim to have success in helping people heal themselves of cancer, Alzheimer, Parkinson, and other chronic illnesses are typically put out of business or have mysterious deaths.

You should talk to people and scan the internet more, trying to find trusted and reputable sources and people with experience in holistic and natural healing. Why not try it? Natural methods do not have side effects. Why would you use medication to eliminate one thing and add several other issues?

Surgeries are risky. How many times have you heard of repeated mistakes? Or are people getting sick or infected from being in the hospital? Or how many surgeries have a person undergone to be healed of a single condition? Why did you suffer when hundreds of less risky and viable options are available to help you combat any health condition while restoring your body to rest and wholeness?

So get educated. Do your research, and learn about these methods and technologies that have been in existence before the pharmaceutical industry. Learn about pioneers' successes in curing AIDS and cancer or other terminal or simple diseases more than three decades ago. There are many banned technologies and supplements in America. For example, when adults have parasites, there are no over-the-counter remedies. You have to get a parasite medicine like those used for animals from a veterinarian. You have heard from the news, even on reputable shows like The Joe Rogan Show, that Ivermectin can heal or even prevent COVID-19 and cancers. However, it was shunned and ridiculed.

The most natural and holistic providers must practice on the down-low, staying within the lines and boundaries governed by the pharmaceutical and medical industry. We should be careful of our utterances and approach when helping people that medicine and surgery failed.

The human population has no idea of this corruption. God forbid news leaks about the success of people getting better and healing. It will only be a short time before they shut down and their lives are in danger. I am always asked, "**Why**

haven't I know this before? Why did I suffer so long when you had the solution all along? I always have to explain that we are prevented to inform of natural healing solutions by government and Big Pharma. It is unfortunate, but I am convinced change will soon be upon us for the better.

In conclusion, clarity, precision, and facts are necessary when choosing the best treatment for you. It does not matter what they say, who is saying it, and why. You must think about yourself first.

Have you ever wondered how someone who has been given three weeks, three months, or three years to live, but when they surround themselves with positive energy and people, they live past their supposed deadline? Every choice is beneficial or detrimental to your well-being, but when you are in a dark place, only facts and weighing your options can help you.

One recurring error patients make entrusting their health decisions to their doctors. Until you try every solution, you cannot fold your arms and ignore the possibility of being healthier with alternative medicine.

To emphasize a point, only accept a treatment alternative with sound knowledge of the facts. It will be regrettable when you find out about a better option you missed because you failed to search and weigh your options.

"Why do they call it 'alternative medicine'? When it is the original medicine that humans have been using for thousands of years?

8

HEALING THE WHOLE BODY

"The Natural healing force within each one of us is the greatest healing force in getting well. Our food should be our medicine. Our medicine should be our food."

— HIPPOCRATES

I needed to add the above quote because most of us have forgotten the ways of our ancestors and health before modern medicine.

Hippocrates, the father of modern medicine, stated that a combination of external factors causes disease. They include lifestyle, diet, the environment, and others. He further said, "View the whole person and not the illness alone.

The power to regain or achieve maximum health lies within you. We often take health for granted until something terrible happens to us. It might be the development of a chronic condition, the onset of a disease, or some other health concern. When a person suffers a health crisis, they often turn to their medical doctor for answers. Their doctor may prescribe medication or recommend surgery to address the issue.

The recommended medical treatment for an illness may save a person's life—I am not disputing this, but it comes with side effects. And in many cases, the side effects far outweigh the benefits of the treatment. Chemo and radiation are good examples of this. Medications and surgery are often a band-aid solution that clearly masks the problem instead of resolving it. That band-aid solution has additional side effects without determining the underlying root cause.

Today, many doctors view the disease without the whole person, and the truth is that when your system is out of balance, you will fall sick.

More is needed to address the physical characteristics of a health issue. As stated above, you must analyze every aspect of yourself, including the emotional and spiritual sides. Everything is energy, and one's unique journey and experience make a mark on them, whether it's physical, spiritual, or emotional. Every aspect must unite to facilitate self-healing from the inside out.

What I mean by inside-out healing is that because we are of energy, and we are using frequencies as energy medicine to change the frequency of another, we are working on an energetic level, the lowest level of our existence. If you take everything and everyone and break them down into molecules, atoms, and particles, we reach energy. Using energy to change energy is very effective. For example let's say you have a pot of hot water. That can be measured in frequencies. Adding the frequency of cold water can change the frequency of the water to warm. This is very quick and effective and the change happens quickly. Unlike outside in healing, we would use a fan for instance to blow on the hot water to change its temperature, (frequency).

The holistic and natural healing method is gaining traction as many seek better and less invasive ways to heal and remain healed. While I do not discredit modern medicine and practices, we can only fully administer healing and expect exceptional results by fully understanding the fundamental origin of the disease and why it is manifesting in the physical.

True healing begins with understanding how a disease can be in the body but is controlled or surviving because of our mind and spiritual acceptance.

Ancient healing approaches are proven methods from those who used them. They birthed modern medicine and, believe it or not, are better at providing total healing to the human body. If we opt for holistic and natural healing, we must be willing to make or let go of tough choices to enjoy the full benefit in the long run.

Many people are skeptical about alternative healing, not because of its potency or the capacity to heal. It is due to misinformation about how the public has interpreted modern medicine. For example, wellness is a state of mind, mental awareness, and emotional state of health, not just the absence of an illness. So, while you pursue a cure for an ailment, you must understand the root cause to prevent the disease from returning. That is holistic wellness and what alternative medicine is all about.

Today, the healthcare industry is grasping the spiritual and emotional self-healing preached by ancient traditions. Total healing must touch all aspects of your human nature—mental, physical, emotional, and spiritual. You cannot heal one without the other, or else the imbalance and illness will remain. Your body's well-being is paramount to enjoying lasting health, and ancient tribes and cultures did that. The ancient tribes viewed the human body as a vessel to realize their vision of perfect health. They believed our mind is an integral part of our body and that no complete self-healing is effective without it. So it is clear that total healing embodies the body, mind, emotions, spirituality, and attitude.

The Mind

Both ancient teaching and modern science agree that the mind is one part of the human body and has the power to influence every other part of the human body. Whether it is your body, thoughts, or emotions, you can activate the ability to heal from the mind.

The brain differs from the mind, but I will address both here. When I was a kid, I wanted to be a brain surgeon. I knew I did not have what it took to go through 7 years of they type of schooling. Contrary to popular belief, I now have over 25 years of experience working with the brain and, in many cases, conducting energetic brain surgeries on my clients.

The mind is a dominant thing. Something that I grew up with is an understanding beyond my years. I understood that positive visualization and energy played a huge role in my success throughout my developing years. I accomplished any goal I set for myself. Where the mind goes, the body goes. When you focus on your health, the body will return to a healthy state. Focus on sickness, and the body will be sick.

It means that when we activate a positive feeling or energy around us, we can feel that positivity. The ambiance surrounds us when we unlock negative power by thought or action. Your emotional response to situations affects your behavior, function, and exhibit. For example, if you keep uttering how tired and drained you are you will start to feel that way? We cannot overlook the mind-body relationship. Step into the power of your mind! Again, the mind is powerful yet misunderstood and under- utilized.

The brain, however, is an organ that drives all of our motor skills, behavior, decisions, reactions, defenses, and survival mechanisms. Stress and trauma cause us to remain in fight or flight or freeze modes. They are working on one's brain, mirroring the brain back to itself so it can simply balance and make the corrections needed to get out of these stuck states of fight or flight or freeze mode. In fight or flight, the person may be angry, jealous, anxious, or suffering from panic attacks. When in freeze mode, the body shuts down the immune system and other systems within the body, such as sleep and detoxing. These are essential functions in any human being.

Balancing the brain eradicates the symptoms, which in turn eliminates the label. The brain does not know titles or tags. The brain knows how to heal everything. Without these advanced brain devices, the brain is just another organ in the body, like bones, nerves, and stomach. The brain and the body must convey with one another. The eyes communicate a cut on your arm that needs healing, and the body takes care of that with the brain's help. A nerve pain alerts the brain to the presence of a problem and directs blood to the affected area for healing.

Furthermore, recognizing that, as humans, you can help your system self-heal faster will enable us to achieve and maintain a healthy state effortlessly. Our ability to reach a wellness point relies on under- standing how the mind (brain) connects with the body.

The brain is an impressive organ. It controls everything, including simple actions like blinking, swallowing, and breathing. The mind is vastly untapped. You can do a lot when you understand that the mind controls the brain. The brain controls the body, and both are connected and work together for optimal health and optimal outcome.

THE BODY

Our bodies can regenerate. Watching a scar fade or seeing a wound heal itself is incredible. We are magical and miraculous and should continue to acknowledge the vessels in which the spirit and brain reside. This container (our body) can thrive under challenging conditions. We must do our part to protect, defend, and prevent it so that we can keep it strong and healthy for years to come. Our bodies do not have to age as we grow, as we can feel and look young. We anticipate things start to break down, and we look and feel worse. That is simply a myth. Many technologies and modalities can reverse the signs of aging and help the brain increase the proteins that support our memory while restoring and regenerating telomeres and stem cells. Once again, I will say this; the human body is perfect, and if we understand that, healing is simple. Millions of people suffer from preventable and chronic diseases because they lack the capability of their bodies. Choices (personal choices) really matter in building the body's self-healing capacity. There are some steps to improve your body's ability;

Strengthen your body through exercises like yoga. Yoga is excellent at sustaining vital energy, boosting your immune system, and increasing your power to focus and alert while enabling you to put your emotions in check. There are other methods, so choose what works best for you. Remember, the body has great potential to self-heal itself naturally, but it depends on our choices.

· · ·

THE SPIRIT

We must acknowledge our spirit body. We are immortal. When we die, we return to an energetic form; without these physical suits, worn in this life-time. The spirit also has energy and should be acknowledged and recognized. Your spirit, like your physical body, deserves love and care. Learn to connect to your childhood spirit. When you bring out your inner child qualities, your spirit will experience happiness and joy, which then triggers endorphins, bringing cellular rejuvenation to the body and brain.

Keeping our spirit strong brings our energy and our frequency up. Conditions, limiting beliefs, people, and stress can squash a person's spirit. Unlike the brain in the body, the spirit continues to exist beyond our lifetime and into the next.

Having a spiritual connection is simply quieting the brain and the body to regain this feeling in your heart, your life's purpose, your happiness, your passions, your joy of being playful, experiencing laughter, and living life to the fullest. When we are children, assuming we grew up in a healthy environment, our spirits are often at their most beneficial and robust. As adults, we forget to get in touch with our spirit, and we often struggle to find answers to our most profound questions. Sitting in a quiet, beautiful space will allow your spirit to shine, showing you the answers you need to heal, be happy, and be healthy. When you remember a time in your childhood when you were thrilled, your spirit shone brightly. I know that after a good rain storm, I loved to play in the mud and the rain and that my child and spirit were living life to the fullest.

When your spirit is happy, bright, and shiny, your cells become full of energy, and the frequencies raise your vibration, which then triggers your telomeres, making cells respond and become healthy, restoring and renewing your brain and body.

Science speaks of the mind, body, and spirit as different entities, but they are not. The connection of the spirit with the mind and body is beautiful. And if we are to enjoy holistic healing or activate the power of self-healing, we cannot do it without the power of the spirit. That is why subscribing to precise medication or treatment is a challenge.

Alternative healing or treatment knows that healing only happens when the three pillars of our existence come together. Only then can you experience a healthy body, mind, and spirit.

Even when the ailment is physical, the root cause emanates from the mind or the spirit. If this is the case, the healing is fast, and disruptions unblocked, then energy flows.

Exercising the spirit is a fundamental part of our healing and is the part of our human self that connects with the life force energy around us. If the spirit is the channel to the energy source, how do we start strong in the spirit?

Exercising the spirit strengthens and activates the divine connection from within to the outside. It allows energy to flow freely, triggering self-healing and causing negative thoughts to dissipate—some steps to help you build a resilient spiritual self.

Spend time around positive energy, fun things, and activities that make you happy, laugh and engage with people, whether family, friends or even strangers outside your home.

Connecting with nature can help you stay spiritually aligned and confident. Nature is a bridge that connects your spirit to the life force. Sometimes, let the sunlight hit your face and cascade down your body, or enjoy the evening breeze on a warm night. Spending time outside in nature opens your senses and fills you with energy.

Stay away from distractions that drain your positive energy. It is necessary. Unending noise that leaves us tired and confused surrounds us. They cause blockages in the spirit and lower our energy frequency.

Discerning your surroundings and people is a great way to strengthen your spirit. Instead of spending time in painful situations, gossiping, or sharing sad and fearful tales, speak well or talk about the positive outcomes that could result from terrible news.

Remaining in the faith and keeping devoted company is one of the best ways to persist in the spirit. There will always be challenges, especially if you have an ailment, you are dealing with, but faith supersedes any problem. It also ensures you stay connected to positive energy from the environment, which hastens your healing and gives a positive perspective to you.

Learn the act of helping or volunteering in your community, starting from your local church, elderly home, or somewhere that needs extra hands. There is power in helping, so powerful that it can turn your situation around. The more we strengthen our spirit; our body and mind receive the same strength. Imagine the smile on a 93-year-old lady with dementia after helping her. Doesn't that feel good?

"Health Is a State Of Complete Harmony Of The Body, Mind and Spirit."

— B.K.S. IYENGAR

9

OUTSIDE FACTORS

"There is never enough time to do everything, but there is always enough time to do the most important thing."

— BRIAN TRACY

nfortunately, as much as we do our best to protect ourselves and make the right choices, there are times when outside factors play a role in our life and health. It is sad when someone gets involved in a car accident and can no longer walk. We will run into many outside factors affecting our health, mind, body, and spirit. The key here is to stay positive, not fear but take action. Regardless of how much we try to protect ourselves, external factors will always affect and change the status of our well-being.

THE TRUTH ABOUT HUMANITY

- The water supply is contaminated
- The food supply is full of poison and mostly fake
- We suppress symptoms with over the counter medicine and prescriptions
- We are nutrient deficient
- We over consume
- We inject our bodies with unnatural substances
- The air is full of pollution
- We are scared of the sun and wear sunscreen
- We don't exercise enough
- We sit in front of technology all day
- We over consume sugar, drugs, alcohol and caffeine
- We are disconnected from our human instincts and nature
- We discount the knowledge of our ancestors
- We live in a corporate slave system

- Our medicine is based on man-made toxic substances
- We lather our bodies in harmful chemicals
- We have unresolved emotional traumas
- We are being intentionally distracted and dumbed down
- We are in a constant state of fight or flight
- We breathe quick and shallow
- Electro-magnetic radiation is all around us
- Our minds are indoctrinated by outside resources
- We don't speak up
- We are being separated and disconnected from each other
- We allow for our government and medical to get away with literally murder
- We don't put our health first
- Most of all, we have lost our spiritual connection

There are outside factors that can be controlled and some that cannot, but by being educated and aware we can take measures to protect ourselves and loved ones.

We have witnessed many miracles of people using their upbeat attitude, determination, hard work, and mindset to overcome unfortunate incidents. We can learn from them, grow from them, and educate ourselves on how to defend and protect ourselves from outside factors occurring in our lives. The choices we make have cause and effect. Being responsible and aware can prevent these outside factors.

Moreover, most clothing, fabrics, furniture, blankets, soaps, lotions, creams, household cleaning supples, detergents, toothpaste are toxic. What? Yes, this was a big shift for me seeing from our clients scan reports showing harmful chemicals, toxins, poisons, pesticides, residue and even radiation.

According to Clinic Compare, out of Britain, they analyzed 179 countries based on information from the World Health Organization. America is the only non-European country to make the top 10 unhealthiest on the list, having the ninth highest rate of obesity in the world — 35% of the adult population is dangerously overweight. It is considered the sickest nation in the developed world, and the USA is one of the worst countries for its diets, foods and fast foods.

Good food and diet are essential for mental health, development, and sustenance on many levels, biologically or psychologically. They define how we act, feel, react, and think about ourselves and our health. Nine hundred, seventy million people suffer from mental health issues worldwide, with anxiety affecting 284 million people. But what is the connection between food and diet, and mental health?

The gastrointestinal tract, also known as the digestive tract or alimentary canal, is a long passage that starts at the mouth and ends at the anus. It is the "second brain." Your second brain is home to billions and billions of good bacteria that control the chem- ical substances dopamine, serotonin, and other neurotransmitters that carry messages to the brain. These good bacteria need fuel (good food) to ensure that neurotransmitter production is normal and okay. The brain perceives this orderliness as happy, joyful, relaxing, and calm, reflected in your behavior. When we eat "bad foods" like sugar, junk food, and processed and packaged foods, we are upsetting the ecosystem, and the brain perceives it otherwise, which affects our mood.

Several studies and reviews have linked mental depreciation to food and diet. A review of 21 studies in 10 countries shows that a diet high in whole grains, fish, low red meat intake, and vegetables or fruits reduced the risk of depression. Another study revealed that people on the Mediterranean diet lowered their risk of depression by 32%. That is huge, but when you stick to foods that upset your internal balance, you indirectly reduce your life force frequency and are prone to ailments. There is no doubt that unhealthy foods and diets are a culprit in mental health issues.

But there are foods that you think are healthy but they are loaded with harmful ingredients. For instance, my favorite dill pickles, although not organic, showed four hazardous toxins as preservatives, causing cancer, memory loss, ADHD, and nerve damage! Can we trust the FDA? What? I continued to go through the store, picking up my favorite things, such as cookies, crackers, and soups, that I thought were healthy but found out these were causing severe toxicity to the body and brain. So even if you are a healthy eater or are a vegan like myself, you have to question and check everything. Most teas, salts, expensive supplements are mostly garbage that actually sets you back!

So what do you do? One of my favorite apps on the phone is a program called YUKA. You can scan the barcode of any food product, cosmetic product, lotion, shampoo, etc., and see the many chemicals that cause cancer, ADHD, memory loss, and more! However, processed foods continue to be on the rise, and even foods that seem healthy and straightforward, without the non-GMO and organic symbols, if you saw the hazardous ingredients in these products, you would surely stop eating them. Do you love McDonalds? I bet you wouldn't eat the burgers there if you knew about adrenochrome.

Most people know that food and diet play a significant role in our health. But you probably do not know that bad food and diet can cause an imbalance that affects your life force energy. You may need to realize the contaminants that exist in our foods.

Even some Himalayan Salts, organic produce and even expensive supplements are mostly garbage that actually sets you back. Stick with NON-GMO and organic to be safe.

What We Put On Our Body

Scan everything you put on yourself. Scan for baby powder! Johnson & Johnson baby products are some of the most toxic but they won't come up on the scan. These big giants can control the information so it doesn't get released. This was a big shift for me seeing from the scans we have of people that fabrics, blankets, clothes are laced with poison, pesticides, residue and even radiation. Do you know that 65% of people are allergic of polyester? That is in most of our clothing? The chemicals on furniture, to cancer causing sunscreens that fabrics, blankets, clothes are laced with poison, pesticides, residue and even radiation. I scanned an organic Hemp lotion that my son used who suffered from dry flaky skin and even that was full of toxins! This was a big awakening for me seeing from the scans run on people. Before I knew of these poisons, unnatural ingredients but didn't realize how much they do effect our health!

What We Drink

Do you know that over "780 million people lack access to clean drinking water"? Additionally, a third of the population lacks proper sanitation, which finds its way into the water sources people consume. In modernized countries, where clean water is available, chemicals like fluoride, toxins, and poisonous chemicals are present in what we drink daily. Certain bottled water won't even freeze! With oceans and water bodies served as dumping sites for plastics and aluminum, they now show up in our bodies and brains, causing significant damage and health issues.

Another factor is the PH of the water. What is the pH of the water you are drinking? Acidic water causes corrosion to metal plumbing, causing metallic components like lead, copper, zinc, and magnesium to leak into drinkable water. These metals increase the pH of the water, causing ailments like gastric reflux, kidney problems, high blood pressure, and cancer.

Alcohol, caffeine, energy drinks, and other stimulants are outside factors that affect the body, mind, and spirit. Alcohol and stimulants affect the neurotransmitters in the brain by preventing them from working correctly. The long-term impact is a heightened feeling of anxiety, worry, stress, and lack of concentration or focus.

What We Are Exposed To By Our Environment

The environment around you is everything. From the air you breathe to where you live (including your neighbors) to the condition of the environment, environmental factors influence your health. Our environment is in bad shape; a statistic from Healthy People states that 23% of all deaths, and 26% of deaths in kids five years old and younger, result from preventable environmental health problems.

Our plants, crops, animals are also being harmed. What's more, the environmental issues, whether human-made, technology-based or natural, are the buildup of decades of mismanagement and neglect.

Think about it for a moment. Your child could be in danger just by playing outside, which is unbelievable. While I urge you to stay optimistic and unafraid and not fear the data that bombard our screens or mail, we must realize that we are not safe from anything.

What We Clean With

Let's talk about our cleaning supplies. Our clients from all over the US get a scan from us thinking they have an allergy or a skin rash, but their bodies show an overload of heavy metals or toxins such as radiation and formaldehyde. It's time to change out your soap, your cleaning products that have harmful toxins and chemicals. Some dryer sheets are even known to cause fibromyalgia!

Even our pets are not safe. They lick everything and ingest poisons from our cleaners and pesticides from the grass and plants.

www.Doterra.com and www.SimpleTruth.com some favorite resources for safe products.

Where We Sleep

When I say everything, I mean everything, including your bed stand, which probably holds your phone and charger and emits harmful EMFs while you sleep. Technology and TVs should not be in the bedroom. Even when off and plugged in you are getting harmful EMFs. Your bedroom should be a sanctuary for sleeping and healing. It is the ONLY time your body can detox and renew itself. Purchase grounding sheets to help your body neutralize the EMFs picked up during the day.

The moment you step out of your house, you are also hit with 5G towers that are very harmful to your cells. Cancer and other autoimmune diseases are triggered more rapidly. God forbid you to live next to one of these towers. Research cell towers near you!

One of my dear friends had a scan done, and they live in a gorgeous mansion, it came up with severe radiation. Little did they know that a 5G tower was built next to them! They could paint their house with toxic lead paint or cover half their house up with a protective tarp? Abnormal cell growth and other life threatening illness is common ground for this situation.

Wonder why more and more men are getting prostate cancer? It's because most men keep their phones in their back pockets. How about women and breast cancer? Many women keep their phone in purses under their arm?

Let's look at your office. Depending on your work environment, many fluorescent lights are installed in the office, also causing damage to your cells.

5G and Electro Magnetic Field effects:

- Reproductive and fertility

- Decreased sperm count, damage to DNA of sperm (within 1 week exposure)
- DNA damage to the heart & brain, heat failure, cardiomyopathy, memory loss, involuntary movement
- Ear damage, dizziness, tinnitus
- Brain damage, brain tumor (salivary gland tumor from cell phone)
- Increases in ALS, Parkinson's, and the mental illnesses
- Causes prostate, breast and skin cancer
- Causes brain fog which sedates us to feeling indifferent, and dumb downs our intelligence
- Nose bleeds

Our phones are 5x higher than what is considered safe by the FDA. The recommended milivolts are 200, where 5G gives off 600-4000 mili volts! It's only about to get worse!

What We Breath

Take a walk on the beach. Look up, and you will see white lines that look like clouds in the sky. They are not clouds. They are toxins scattered in the skies called Chemtrails. Whether you have heard about it, let's state the facts first. Chemtrails are not contrails; do not be deceived by the government and so-called environmentalists. Chemtrails are killing the environment, polluting our natural habitats (water bodies, flora, and fauna of the forests), land, and people. They affect rainfall, increase humidity and heat, and cause respiratory illnesses, mental stress, depression, weak muscles, and weakened immune systems. They contain harmful chemicals dangerous to humans, plant life, and animals. What is next for the earth's population if our air contains chemical toxins? Weather reporters are under gag orders to not report known Chemtrails that control our weather. Geo-engineering, strips the sunlight reaching earth, adding particles and chemicals to atmosphere, one reason to help reduce global warming using Aluminum and Sulfur which directly causes asthma. They are also shooting salt particulates in the air to make it rain. The salts reach our soil which is bad for crops and ruin drinking water. All drinking water since 1990 show spikes for chemicals.

Where do we turn? How do we protect ourselves? The goal is to protect, prevent, and educate yourself in your home and work environment to reduce and eliminate these harmful toxins and EMFs.

Learn more here:

http://knowingthetruth.com/smart-meters-emf-health-hazard

http://www.RadiationReport.com/smartmeters

However, DO NOT FEAR! Being aware of the problems and educating ourselves about them will equip us with the right tools to protect and defend ourselves. That is right! We have to take proactive measures to stop, protect and detox from these.

Get scanned, tested, scan everything you put on or in you. Research cell towers near you, use EMF protective devices.

Some of my favorites are https://airestech.com/ or https://bodyalign.com

Parasites

These are tiny living organisms that depend on other living organisms to survive. They are every- where in our bodies, foods, environments, and with other people within our social circle.

While some are harmless, others are not so welcoming and cause diseases that affect your immune system, well-being, and life. Parasites can be defined as fungus and bacteria, or anything with a host. They are basically the root of every disease. 90% of parasites come from pets and our water.

However, humans always have a solution – vaccination. The question is does being vaxxed or unvaxxed change your susceptibility to getting an infection? Are vaccines doing more harm or less to the human body?

There are facts we should remember about these tiny invaders. They multiply over time – they never wholly die away or disappear. You are their host and a growth habitation.

The more they multiply in your body, the more active your immune system is to keep them in check. It means that, at some point, your immune system is overworking itself. As we get older it becomes harder.

The more compromised your immune system, the likelihood you will get an autoimmune disease, and eventually they burrow into your tissue where cysts grow beyond control, they get infected and you get diagnosed with cancer.

Detox parasites for 6 weeks, then 1-2 times per year. We consume far too much food and absorb far too many toxins. Parasite cleansing can be accomplished with frequency healing, or supplements/herbs like Fenben, Ivermectin, clove, wormwood and black walnut to name a few.

Pharmaceuticals

These are highly toxic and our body reacts to them like poisons, which cause inflammation and many other side effects. The pharmaceutical industry is like an organized criminal group and the leading cause of death in the US and the world. And one wonders why the government is not doing enough to clamp down on their activities. The World Health Organization controls many governments.

Some Statistics Over The Years:

In 2017, according to the DOJ, of the $3.7 billion in judgments and settlements, $2.4 billion concerns the healthcare industry. Everyone was roped in, including physicians, pharmacies, hospitals, drug companies, and labs.

In 2018, the settlements and judgments were $2.8 billion

In 2021, according to the National Health Care Fraud Enforcement action, more than 138 defendants were charged, 42+ licensed medical professionals were charged more than $1.4 billion of the alleged loss, and 12+ million prescribed opioid pills.

According to an article in Washington Post in 1998, 2 million Americans become sicker annually from properly prescribed medication. One hundred six thousand die from adverse reactions to it. In 2015, the FDA placed prescription drugs as the fourth leading cause of death in the US.

According to the World Health Organization, 10% of the global pharmaceutical industry trades in counterfeit drugs, which is a turnover of $21 billion. Countries like China, Vietnam, and the Philippines have the highest recorded incidents, up to 48% and 1% of these drugs sold in the US.

The stats are staggering, but big pharmaceuticals have killed more people today than all the world wars and terrorism. You do the math!

Every day, innocent people die; while many may not believe it, keep in mind that a product is not safe simply because it has been proven, certified, or tested to be safe.

Pharmaceuticals are unnatural chemicals. It slowly causes the body to build toxins in the pancreas, gall- bladder, and liver. Gradually, they began to shut down. People often use 5 to 15 different pharmaceutical drugs. Seniors typically take anywhere between 10 and 30 prescriptions. I have even seen clients who brought in large Ziplock bags, filled with supplements and prescriptions, showing me what they took for breakfast, lunch, and dinner. It is outrageous, and at what point will the doctor or pharmaceutical company opt for other options that cleanse rather than download it with more prescription drugs?

How on earth can the body process all of these plastic capsules, colored dyes, and toxic chemicals? It is enlightening when I approach the doctors who prescribe these medications and many overlooked contradictions that could be fatal. Often, working with clients, I ask the doctors which medication they must stay on and prevent them from having to take any of them.

Again, like our government, Big Pharma has a money-making agenda. Educate yourself on herbs and how essential oils are 50% more potent. These are excellent replacements to help heal just about anything. One of my favorite sources is www.Doterra.com because of their purity and ethics.

Finally, as more people focus on prevention rather than treatment, holistic measures is the solution. The pharmaceutical industry sees this as a threat as funding drops, profits drop, and many people do not receive money for doing anything. Alternative medicine is a threat to the big boys, but it is time we open our eyes to the dangers the industry is causing.

Smoking & Vaping

The most common trend among Americans is vaping. I have to admit; this is a lot more pleasant than being around someone who is a cigarette or cigar smoker. I don't have to take on secondhand smoke and be at risk for my health. However, it is discouraging that 9 out of 10 people can't withstand 30 minutes without vaping. Like Starbucks Coffee defines as a "lifestyle," vaping is the next unhealthy trend.

The dangers of smoking or inhaling artificial smoke to one's health go beyond the cigarette. As ongoing campaigns on smoking hit hard on the mainstream, it has reduced, but like the Pharma industry, when one door closes, another opens, and we have e-cigarettes and vaping.

According to the CDC, tobacco is the leading cause of preventable deaths in the US. With over 40 million adults still inhaling tobacco smoke, it will take a severe effort to clamp down. Smoking affects every organ in the human body, including the immune system. It makes smokers prone to respiratory diseases like coughs, chest congestion, cancers, and heart-related problems. Despite the continuous changes in the law to reduce smoking, young people still indulge in it.

Statistics on smoking

13% will die from chronic lung obstruction. 25% of male and 26% of female smokers will develop lung cancer.

81% of adults in their 30s and older will die of cancer of the lungs, trachea, and bronchus.

The CDC expects 236,740 new lung cancer cases and 130,180 deaths from lung cancer in 2022.

Are you part of the statistics?

Vaping

Many believe vaping is a way to save the population from the dangers of tobacco smoke. And I am here thinking about how inhaling aerosol is better than burning tobacco. And with over 2 million vaped teens in the US in 2022, vaping also hurt your health. If it is "good," it should not have any side effects.

- Vaping destroys mouth cells and increases the risk of gum disease.
- Vaping causes wounds to heal slower as cells cannot quickly repair themselves because they are weak.
- Vaping causes respiratory problems like lung obstructions and damage to lung tissue. Vapers are prone to cardiovascular problems and cancers as vapors can irritate the lungs and trigger cancer-forming cells.
- Vapes contain nicotine that causes users to become addicted to them.
- Because most vapers share instruments, infection can spread.

Vaping is unsafe, and with short-term and long-term effects on crucial body organs, it is lackadaisical to ignore it for the fun of it. The CDC has confirmed 2,711 hospitalized cases and 60 deaths from vaping. While the short-term effect of vaping is known, the long-term impact is still under research. I hope it will not be detrimental to our young ones when the news breaks out when they are old. Vaping is like smoking tobacco, and with more than 2,600 registered cases of acute lung disease, why would anyone think otherwise? Furthermore, the lungs of vapers and pets or people exposed to vaping smoke showed increased inflammation, sore throats, coughs, and dry mouth. Another study reported that vaping increases labored breathing as long as tissues are fatigued and damaged. Additionally, 30% of vapers are likely to develop asthma. 60% will develop obstructive pulmonary disease.

Whether vaping will cause cancer, heart disease, or increase your chance of a heart attack is a study for the long term, as vaping is still new. It's best not to start it because it's not easy to stop. My mother died of cancer, not in the lungs, however. She had been a smoker since she was a young adult, and it was very difficult for her, even with her strong willpower, to stop. It eventually caught up to her. I have a lot of compassion and empathy for those trying to quit. If I only had the tools, I have today to help detect and facilitate healing in a whole new way. It is not an easy road. However, there are plenty of practical and natural methods available to help.

"It's easy to let external factors define us, especially the unfavorable ones, but only if we let them. Keep fighting & the unfavorable will become favorable."

— SHAHENSHAH HAFEEZ KHAN

10

STRESS IS THE NUMBER ONE CAUSE OF DISEASE & ILLNESS

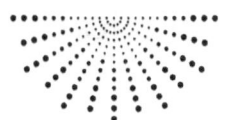

"There is never enough time to do everything, but there is always enough time to do the most important thing."

— BRIAN TRACY

Stress is the number one cause of disease and illness. Let's say this again. Stress is the NUMBER 1 cause of disease and illness! We create our own stress. We are responsible for feeling stress. We allow stress to happen to us. It is a choice. Even so called recreational things like Social Media causes information overload causing the body stress. Our phones cause stress.

Now beyond that our own mind is creating more stress with all our thoughts!

Check out some of these facts:

According to the Stress in America survey results, adults continue to report high-stress levels, with many reporting that their stress has increased in the last year. The American Psychological Association

75% of adults reported moderate to high levels of stress in the previous month, and nearly half reported an increase in pressure during the last year - The American Psychological Association

According to the National Institute of Mental Health, one out of every 75 people has panic disorder.

Stress is a top concern for us teens between ninth and twelfth grade, and psychologists say if they don't learn healthy ways to manage stress now, it could be profound long-term health implications (American Psychological Association)

80% of workers feel stress on the job, nearly half say they need help in learning how to manage stress, and 42% say their co-workers need such help as well—American Institute of Stress

Stress levels in the workplace are raising, with 6 in 10 workers in major global economies experiencing increased workplace stress. China, at 86%, has the highest rise in workplace stress—the Regis group.

Alarmingly, 91% of adult Australians feel stress in at least one crucial area of their lives. Almost 50% feel stressed about one part of their life – Life Line Australia.

These statistics don't even consider the recent pandemic, which has left many people globally with elevated trauma and stress levels. Social anxiety, panic attacks, depression, and intense stress have increased among all races and all age groups.

Since I began my alternative therapy journey, I realized that many ailments people deal with are stress based, impacting their personal and professional lives. In addition to the statistics above, medical practitioners agree that 90% of visits are stress related. People worry about job pressures, work overload, colleague stress, money, family, sleep, poor nutrition, and relationships. Even more disheartening is that more than half of these numbers are neck-deep in focus, destroying healthy relationships and families.

Understanding Stress And Your Health

Stress is a psychological pain that presses our insides, giving us that feeling of a tight squeeze, which is detrimental to our well-being. We all know stress is wrong, but are you aware that it is the root cause of many ailments? Why? Stress affects the immune system, lowering its ability to tackle diseases and exposing us to everything. As a believer in life force energy and a propagator of energy balance for self-healing and wholeness, stress disconnects us from alignment with our life force. This distortion causes fear and doubt, which negatively influence our minds. Do you suffer from sleep deprivation, poor diet, anxiety, fear, chronic illness, or low immunity? You are stressed. Are you uncertain of what life has in store for you? Are you indecisive about the next step in your life? Are you tense and afraid of situations even before you face them? You are stressed. Uncertainty surrounds us; we live in fear and suffer from inflammation and bouts of anger.

. . .

MANAGING Stress for Self-Healing

Our bodies can heal themselves; it is an innate ability that every human was born with, the ability to fight infection or repair injuries. But when stressed, we can help the body heal by partaking in activities that boost our mood, mental drive, and immunity. While the body can do amazing stuff at sustaining itself, we should pay attention to our doctor's or healer's advice to have a sound body, mind, and spirit. The doctor can suggest ways to boost your body's natural immunity, but below are some ways.

Use Guided Meditation.

If you love meditating but find yourself drifting into your problems, you need a guide. With guided meditation, the guide helps you stay focused, thereby getting the best results. If you cannot afford a guide, there are videos online and free guides ready to offer a helping hand to people that need it.

Practice Deep Breathing.

When we stress, we fail to breathe effectively, and most people are short of breath, panting, or suffer panic attacks. On the other hand, stress depletes our energy source, and deep breathing increases energy levels, bringing our system to a place of harmony.

Why is deep breathing important? Most of the time, we only use 5.6% of the oxygen inhaled. Even though the lungs retain some oxygen, deep breathing allows us to sink into our bodies and creates a relaxing atmosphere in and around us. Deep breathing reduces the control of the sympathetic nervous system. This system handles how our body perceives danger, and by breathing deeply, we slow our heart- beat, stabilize blood pressure, and beat down stress effects to the minimum. Deep breathing also improves clarity and activates your parasympathetic nervous system, which helps you manage stress and other mental issues.

Exercise and Dieting

How you respond to stress is a powerful force to combat this condition. When stressed, our bodies release stress hormones such as cortisol and adrenaline to prepare us for flight, fight or freeze. You are what you eat. You are destroying your health if you eat junk, processed, and packaged foods. We discussed how food and diet affect communication between neurotransmitters and the brain.

When you exercise, chemical hormones like endorphins flood your system, picking us out of that grim and stressful situation by improving your mood and activating the body's painkillers. These chemicals, while they help us manage stress, dampen our moods and deactivate the body's self-healing capability. So, with proper nutrition and exercise, you build a solid system and strengthen the body's natural healing process.

Reduce News, Newspapers, and Social Media

This tip isn't for kids and young adults only. Adults should learn to manage screen time, whether it's for news or social media. It has nothing new to offer, only negative stories to create fear and stress. I have not watched the news or read the newspaper or news radio my entire life and I have never been called out of touch. Anything newsworthy, trust me you will hear about. There is so much face news out there you have to be very careful as well. Facebook and other social apps literally feed of the listening through your phone and computer. So now you know why if you were taking about raking the leaves, a rake will show up for you to purchase. This is not by accident and designed that way. Even our political and religious views can be skewed without our knowing through what is posted and shared. It is depressing. We see painful information before any good one. But you can read watch positive things that inspire and educate you in a non-stressful way. Or take up a hobby that keeps you busy and away from negative distractions.

Reduce Screen Time

This tip isn't for kids and young adults only. Adults should learn to manage screen time, whether it's for news or social media. It has nothing new to offer. It is depressing. We see painful information before any good one. The same goes with social media, but you can read that favorite book, watch nature, or take up a hobby that keeps you busy and away from negative distractions.

Build Healthy Relationships

Human beings survive by interacting with creatures; we need people to complete that circle. Enjoying a shared space or activity with friends and family builds good memories, relationships, and a sense of belonging. Good relationships reduce stress, over thinking, and loneliness.

So the next time your body starts to ache or your lower back starts to sense pain, question the emotional trigger. Your body is trying to tell you something. The symptoms that you feel are communicating that we are stressed and injured. Unhealthy cells release chemicals that activate nerves and send signals to your brain. Your brain registers these unpleasant symptoms that you feel. The more your cells are stressed, the more or how intense your discomfort will be. Everything in your body is connected, creating a domino effect from the brain to the body.

If you notice you feel worse after talking with a friend, make note of that as they may be brining your energy down and therefore you need to limit contact with that person or create some boundaries.

Sleep

Sleep relaxes the mind, body, and spirit and ensures that the tripartite nature of man remains in harmony and the life force energy is balanced. Sleep deprivation is absolute and affects people more than they realize. You may feel threatened, afraid, para- noid, or even psychotic if you suffer from a sleeping problem. Furthermore, anxiety, depression, panic attacks, and suicidal tendencies are symptoms of a lack of sleep.

Sleep and mental health are connected. Millions of people, especially Americans, have a massive sleep problem. Unfortunately, the situation worsened with the lockdown, unemployment, and isolation from friends and family. Let's understand one fact: sleep deprivation and insomnia are symptoms of mental illness or used to determine the onset of one. According to a study published in Sleep Medicine 2021, of the 22,330 participants that took part in the research, one in three has symptoms of clinical insomnia, and 20+% met the benchmark for insomnia. Why is sleep an important factor in creating balance? In chapter 9, we discussed how the mind works with the brain. If the brain delivers the wrong messages, your mind acts that way. For example, if the brain senses fear, it senses a letter to the mind, and the body works on it. With this ideology, sleep deprivation creates a disconnection that the brain interprets negatively, affecting its normal function. Proper sleep increases cognitive abilities, attention span, focus, learning capability, memory, and the ability to perceive cheerful ambiance and deal with stress. However, getting a good night's sleep depends on other factors, including what you eat, where you live, and your social circle. Are you doing it right?

So the next time your body starts to aches or your lower back starts to sense pain, question the emotional trigger. Your body is trying to tell you something. The symptoms that you feel are communicating that we are stressed and injured. Unhealthy cells release chemicals that activate nerves and send signals to your brain. Your brain registers these unpleasant symptoms that you feel. The more your cells are stressed, the more or how intense your discomfort will be. Everything in your body is connected, creating a domino effect from the brain to the body.

The True Source of Pain & Suffering

We all have experienced unresolved tensions and issues with people. It manifests as physical pain and illness. Get rid of all bitterness, anger, rage, hate and negative feelings towards someone or yourself. How? Try to forgive and let go of emotional baggage. Do it for you if you can't do it for them, as you will be the one rotting in the poison that it will cause you. Remove things in your home that might be linked to negative.

Protect your home from negative energies, entities: Spirit in the name of and by the authority of the almighty God, my Lord and Savior Jesus Christ, and the Holy Spirit, begone."

Amen!

"It's easy to let external factors define us, especially the unfavorable ones, but only if we let them. Keep fighting & the unfavorable will become favorable."

— SHAHENSHAH HAFEEZ KHAN

11

YOUR SUPPORT SYSTEM

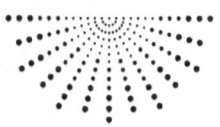

"It's not the load that breaks you down, it's the way you carry it."

— LOU HOLTZ

*I*f you are okay with alternative or holistic medicine, chances are your family is against it because many people still do not understand how it works. Natural healing needs more awareness in our society. If you choose the holistic, self-healing, and alternative healing process, you cannot go through it alone. You need help, and loved ones must be present to help you understand, encourage, and nudge you when the days are dark and gloomy. Every year, millions of people suffering from chronic or terminal illnesses opt for integrated medical choices. While watching a loved one suffer is hard, you must also support their options, as it will ease their healing and recovery process.

I will be honest; I have come face-to-face with frustrated, angry, and resentful family members who are bitter about the treatment not working as they thought. I quickly tell them it is a repair, restoration, and healing process. At some point, these patients have spent years swallowing prescription drugs. The system needs cleansing and a thorough education on the emotional impact of the new treatment they chose. Aside from all the worries, families and friends want to support their loved ones in times of trouble. Dealing with a health crisis is hard, but as many people incline their hearts to be natural and alternative approaches, a unified support system is an essential pillar of healing and recovery. In this chapter, I will discuss having a sound support system.

Why do you need a support system?

When a loved one is diagnosed with a disease or has a symptom of a terminal illness like cancer, their life changes immediately. A rush of emotions, mostly fear and disbelief, are relatable expressions.

However, opting out of an alternative or holistic approach is a different ball game. It involves lifestyle changes, diet changes, attitude changes, and other aspects that friends and family will not understand. While you need their support as you struggle to gain control of yourself and your health, you also need positive people around you. And the best way to get everyone on board with your supposedly unified support system is by educating them. Remember, there will be some affirmative and some disagreements, but the decision is yours. Anyone who disagrees with your decision has two options: learn about it and support you, or wait for you at the end of your recovery.

Additionally, their disagreement is not hated. They are worried and want the best for you. So be nice and do not take it too hard. Furthermore, the external voices will be loud. Yes, they will, and it is natural to want to accept their choice, but you must remember that you are the one that needs healing and not them.

. . .

How to talk **about your choice of healing?**

- Remember, you are the one with the disease, but be nice.
- Be assertive and not aggressive when voicing your reasons for choosing this healing technique.
- Try to find a system that educates your support system.
- Enlighten them about the way the disease makes you feel.
- Let them understand that you value their opinion but draw the line.

Support systems are the best way to heal, especially when dealing with a chronic or terminal disease that has lingered for years. While it is normal to see a loved one overreact, you cannot blame them for trying to keep you alive. When educating yourself, you need to inform the people around you. Often, your friends and family will not know, understand, or even accept new information and concepts because they believe in only one way. They don't want to change, and they don't want to open their minds to other possibilities. That is okay. Give them compassion and love, and find people who can be a part of your support system.

Educate Your Support System

Often, I hear people trying to heal in alternative ways and getting condemned for their choices. They are fear-driven, which causes you more fear, which causes more pain. As you set out to educate them, keep the communication lines open and without prejudice, give them a chance to express their pros or cons of the treatment, and appreciate their honesty.

Set Strict Boundaries

Carrying an illness is a burden, and while our loved ones feel they understand, you alone can truly express how you feel and why you chose an option. However, after educating your support system, anyone who voices negativity does not deserve to be around you. It would be best if you had positive energy. People who exude that energy will help you scale through the difficulties toward attaining the physical, emotional, and mental healing you deserve.

FIND EXTERNAL SUPPORT Groups

If you do not want friends and family journeying with you, there are support groups that allow you to heal and recover without castigating your decisions. Check through your local directory or the clinic. You will find one that checks the boxes for you.

During your healing time, you must surround your- self with people who support your decisions and plans. If they do not, you can quietly dismiss them and tell them you will reach out to them when you recover completely.

Recovery is multi-layered, and you must have the proper support system throughout your new-found healing journey.

> "SOMETIMES WE NEED someone to simply be there. Not to fix anything or do anything in particular, but just to let us feel we are supported and cared about."
>
> — TINY BUDDHA

12

TAKING ACTION AND STICKING TO THE PLAN

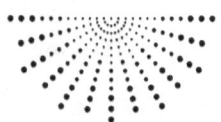

"Small deeds done are better than great deeds planned."

— PETER MARSHALL

*T*ake charge to promote your healing and wellness.

How often have you created a plan but never followed it? It is the small deeds that make all the difference. When you focus on your health, you cannot eliminate all the negatives. It is a gradual process that begins with understanding.

Accepting that there will be changes is the first step to sticking to a plan. If you cannot bear the transition, you are not mentally prepared to follow through on your goal. A lifestyle change includes forgoing certain habits, even if they are good. If a practice is not adding value to your life, it is better than you thought.

Now for the more challenging part, which is sticking to the plan? When dealing with a life-threatening disease or illness, everyone wants to get involved, and everyone will have an opinion. What is right for you? That is where you take time to sit quietly and go within. The answer will reside within you, and you must trust and stick with it.

While we still need to fully understand why we find it hard to take the next step, it is an obligation to proceed. If you still find it hard to stick to the plan, check the following areas:

Are your goals clear enough?

What is stopping you? Subtle fear is like cutting a tree and leaving the stump on the ground. It will grow back. Deal with any anxiety so that the results will not be short-term.

How confident are you about the decision? Being optimistic about the decision ensures you are willing to follow through regardless of the hiccups, hindrances, and challenges.

Are your goals manageable?

Setting manageable plans will set you up for success. It will give you the confidence to forge ahead and want to cross the finish line.

Be accountable.

Accountability is the only way to avoid derailing as you make the process. If you cannot do it independently, invite your support system to ensure you remain on track.

Be bold and take a stand.

Don't let others influence your decision, pressure you, or instill fear in your mind. The only two cases where we could have had more success were when the client kept switching from our protocol to other protocols and back again after they worsened. It is your life, your body, and your decision. So stick to it! Be sure to inform all those who know you, respect your wishes and keep their thoughts and opinions to themselves unless otherwise asked.

"You can either step forward into growth or step backward into safety."

— ABRAHAM MASLOW

13

EVERYTHING CAN BE HEALED

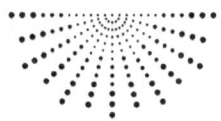

"Healing is an art. It takes time. It takes practice. It takes love."

— DOHTA MAZA

I don't know about you, but for the longest time, I thought we lived with the same liver, heart, and organs throughout our entire life. Little did I know that our bodies constantly regenerate every cell in them? If you have a cut, your body is intelligent enough to restore the cells that create the skin to heal.

Our entire body rebuilds itself in less than two years, ninety-eight percent of it in less than 365 days. Every cell in your body eventually dies and is replaced by new cells. Every day is a unique opportunity to build a whole new body!

- DNA renews itself every two months.
- Your liver rebuilds itself in 6 weeks.
- The lining of your stomach rebuilds itself in 5 days. Your brain rebuilds itself in 1 year. Your body builds a whole new skeleton in 3 months.
- Your blood renews itself every four months. Your skin rebuilds itself in 1 month.

Demonstrating using light and frequency to help repair organs and tissues. Hole in the heart, (no holes). The body can heal. Just because the medical doctor says it is not true, doesn't mean it's true. Even limbs can regrow just like the tail of a lizard with ultra high frequencies.

How exciting is that? So you are not doomed. You have every ability and possibility to change the direction of your health. Keep in mind that your immune system is the secret. You can fight off any disease or illness if your immune system is robust. Everything has an energetic vibration, and when your body, brain, and spirit experience lower vibrations, such as stress, anger, depression, and anxiety, your immune system begins to deteriorate. Your immune system is responsible for detoxing.

Parasites, candida, toxins, heavy metals, nutrient deficiencies, clogged liver and dehydration are the primary things that make you sick. These are the things that western medicine gleefully ignores and most people have no idea about.

Aging does not equal disease. Most people are just chronically dehydrated and full of worms. The human body is extremely durable. It's a miracle suit that adapts and allows us to stay alive in the harshest of environments. There is a fail safe fall back called fasting that can reverse disease and renew the body. There are many good natural solutions to help us on our journey. All disease is reversible and completely curable.

You cannot detox well if you do not get proper sleep. If pathogens build up in your body and overload your immune system, then your immune system cannot do its job. If your liver, pancreas, and gall- bladder are overwhelmed with pathogens and toxins, then they cannot do their job and detoxify you. Toxins cannot leave the body if your lymphatic system is clogged. Cells can regenerate to be healthy if we reduce stress, pathogens, and unhealthy behavior.

Why have I never been sick even after caring for over 3000 positive-tested COVID-19 clients? And no way did I get the vaccination. I saw what was in them through my clients. The dangerous cocktail that goes into our brain and body is appalling, and my number one priority is my immune system. I ensure I eat right, get proper rest, keep my stress factors low, ensure my gut is healthy, and my attitude is optimistic. In the split second of even remotely not feeling good, I decided not to go there. I don't even allow it as a thought to come into my realm of reality.

If your frequency and energy are high and vibrating above 500 decibels, then your brain and body can overcome nearly anything that comes its way. In high-frequency energy, disease and illness cannot exist. Lower frequencies are when disease and condition attach themselves to our cells. That is why it's vital to move through whatever difficulty or stress you are experiencing, focus on the lesson, and be grateful and joyous about your health and life. Similarly, it is not necessarily true when people say they have a genetic disposition to get Alzheimer's or Parkinson's. All these elements play a primary role in each individual's health potential.

The gut contains eighty percent of our immune system. Keep it healthy, and your immune system is ready for defense. The immune system is very sophisticated. Thank goodness we have been exposed to too many microbes and toxins, which help build our immunity.

Vibrational Energy / Frequency Healing

Modern medicine believes people fall sick because they have subjected themselves to infection through precise means. Vibrational medicine thinks that when our energy frequencies are imbalanced, we open ourselves up for diseases and health issues to develop. This philosophy recognizes that everything in nature contains energy, even in dark matter, and that humans can travel or fall into any of these vibrational frequencies as we do our daily chores.

For example, have you ever gotten so angry and stomped out of your home, then saw a rainbow and it calmed you down? You stop suddenly for seconds or minutes. You feel calm and at peace as all the anger dissipate. You connected to that happy energy frequency and felt the rainbow raise your vibration.

I know this sounds crazy, but there are people, places and things that elevate our energy, making us feel better, no matter the problem.

Our bodies, too, can connect to the different vibrational energy frequencies and trigger a self-healing process. Alternative treatments like Frequency Heal- ing, Reiki, and KI use energy frequencies to initiate healing.

Remember when I said I understood energy at a young age? I have never been sick a day in my life. I understand energy and feeling good is to feel God, feeling gratitude vibrates at 750 decibels and love at 500. So if we strive to keep our energy above 500, disease and illness cannot attach itself to something that vibrates that fast. Lower energies like fear, hate, jealousy, guilt, shame all vibrate very slowly and living in that energy makes us feel bad and lowers our vibrational energy, putting us at risk for sickness.

Below are a few examples of healing frequencies for the human body. We have thousands of frequencies for everything you can think of.

- At 285 Hz, cells and tissues heal at the frequency, and the body feels rejuvenated.
- 396 Hz—at this frequency, our mental state is free of fear and guilt, making room for higher-vibration emotions and calmness.
- 417 Hz—difficult situations resolve themselves. Cells undergo repairs, DNA heals, and we experience a sense of vibrant consciousness.
- 639 Hz—this vibration energy frequency connects to our hearts and allows us to love, self-love, and love others. It helps one to love selflessly.
- 741 Hz: At this frequency, the cells exposed to electromagnetic radiation are cleansed and healed. It also triggers a mental sense of empowerment and the drive to create their desired reality. Your intuition is on alert.
- 963 Hz – At the energy frequency, the pineal gland is activated and realigns the body to its original state.

There are many other vibrational energy frequencies for healing; we learn how to tune them and trigger a self-healing system.

SKYE ANGELOU

Scary Fact: Governments and various security apparatuses have used music to control us using music. All the music of the West that's based on the standard 12-tone scale is used for the management of crowds as well as thought control. **Read More Here:**

https://globalnews.ca/news/4194106/440-hz-conspiracy-music/

Understanding Vibrational Frequency From Quantum Physics Viewpoint

However, your ability to self-heal can only occur when you are in alignment with the life force and intentionally in tune with your purpose. The Egyptians used vibrations as a healing medium, and various scientists and mathematicians, including Pythagoras, Nikola Tesla, and others, recognized the power of vibration and its ability to heal, restore, and rejuvenate the human body, mind, soul, and spirit.

Every object on earth has a vibrational frequency, and when you are in tune with it, you feel a connection. Likewise, our cells and organs vibrate at different frequencies and resonate with certain frequencies too.

Imagine this: have you ever wondered why certain music or sounds affect you so much? It is because you tuned in to the frequency. These external forces can be anything: your environment, friends, food, dieting, social circle, and many more. Lower frequencies are not good for us; they make us moody, sickly, and downcast, but higher frequencies make us come alive, bubbly, and happy. There are so many things that affect our vibrational frequency, and there are simple acts that increase our frequency and trigger self-healing, restoration, calmness, and longevity.

What you think about you bring about.

Everything you think, say, wish for, or feel sends a frequency out into the universe and then returns to you. These emotions affect you and impact you either way. If you are always in the negative zone, feeling downcast and harboring emotions like anger, sadness, fear, low self-esteem, and discouragement, you will feel that way because your thoughts have programmed an atmosphere around you to enable these feelings. However, if you transform these thoughts into positive ones, you will enjoy better days.

For example, if you are always afraid of doctor visits or test results, turn that fear into positive affirmations like "I am healing" or "Everything works according to my thoughts and I have the power."

It is crucial to understand that the quality of your thoughts can change even in the toughest adversity. It is not a magic wand but a gradual process that will eventually change everything you believe. I believe in positive thoughts and the power to change my world using positive affirmations. My advice is to think positively at all times.

People

Negative energy is contagious, and if you surround yourself with people in this category, you will embody the bad energy they carry. It is easy to attract negativity because positive vibes and people are one object with the power to alter our vibrational frequencies for the better or worse. The people you keep in your circle are crucial to your growth. If your social circle is dark, complaining, and ungrateful, so will you.

In the chapter "Your Support System," we talked about choosing the right team to surround yourself with during your healing and recovery journey. It was intentional, as negative vibes are counterproductive to your success, and you do not want such vibes. For example, if you have friends who cannot see that the glass is half full, it is time to detox, as such attitudes will cause a decline in your frequency and dampen your mood.

I tell my clients, "Detox your circle." Everybody cannot be around you if they are not introducing something positive to you, and vice versa. The law of attraction is real; do not get sucked into other people's dark holes.

Music

In case you missed it, music therapy is a profitable field, and for men and women using this channel to evoke healing, the results are incredible, long-last- ing, and satisfying. Music is powerful and settles deeply into our souls, spirits, and minds. It can elicit emotional responses that you either ignored or were unaware of. Additionally, music can stimulate, alter, relax, heal, and transform.

When it comes to transformation, the lyrics of the music are just as important as the music itself. Lyrics that are too loud, disorganized, and meaningless will have the opposite effect on your emotions. They might worsen your problem. For example, imagine being stressed or depressed while listening to music about death, unforgiveness, murder, sadness, neglect, dishonor, and the like. How would you feel? So the lyrics are significant as you attract what you feel into your space, life, and environment.

Aside from balancing the body's vibrational energy, music or good sound improves cardiovascular health, mood, orientation, cognitive ability, and brain function; boosts immunity; triggers cell healing and restoration, and reduces pain. Thanks to technology, we have access to millions of playlists that can boost our lives, well-being, and health at no extra cost. If you feel misaligned or out of tune, soak yourself in the healing power of music.

What You See

The eyes are the window to the soul, mind, and spirit. What are you looking at? Technology is a central pillar of our lives, and TVs or media systems are a favorite way to relax, catch up on the fun, or just lounge lazily at home. However, it turns out that what you watch, read, and allow yourself to see affects your entire being. One study showed that, although watching TV in-creases alertness, it makes the brain less focused. Aside from the above, what you watch affects your temperament, mood, and behavior. Whether you agree or not, what you see sips into your mind, soul, and spirit.

Unfortunately, we fail to realize that while we cannot control what is before us, we can choose not to indulge in it. For example, it is thrilling to watch horror or suspense movies that keep you on the edge of your seat, but have you thought of the aftermath of those scenes, reactions, and events? We're guessing you didn't. Anyway, your brain builds a reality around what you put before it. Let me explain it this way: if you surround yourself with healthy images, you act better, whether in your attitude or mannerism. How-ever, these images, pictures, and scenes affect our vibrational frequency, fueling emotions beyond our control and spiraling us into the depths of despair.

Atmosphere

The universe is the blanket that surrounds us. It contains the life force and energy we need to stay balanced and "alive." Our vibrational frequencies need a seamless, unhindered path to remain connected to us, and anything that disrupts this flow affects us adversely. Look at it this way. Imagine that you walk into a home and everything is in place. The environment is clean, uncluttered, and beautiful, and you can see the elegance that went into it. How do you feel?

Now let us imagine the same process in a dirty, unkempt, and disorganized space. The first thing that happens is that your eyes are everywhere, you do not know where to start, your heart beats faster, and other sensory organs react differently as fear suddenly creeps into your space.

Do you feel like this too?

Everything in the universe follows a pattern. The trees are where they should be, the mountains are where they should be, and the rivers are flowing as they should. However, we destroy everything when we disrupt this system.

The word is mighty than the sword.

Utterances/Words

The tongue is one of the most powerful organs in the human body and can make or mar our lives as we know them. Words have altered history. We cannot over-emphasize the power of spoken words, whether in our lives or surroundings. Words are how we define ourselves, and our minds recognize them as power points to build us. For example, if you use derogatory comments to describe yourself as fat, worthless, useless, stupid, incompetent, and weak, that is how you will become a reality. However, the wrong words also shift your vibrational frequency as you claim them unintentionally. We function at higher frequencies, and to remain in that realm, stop using your words and putting your- self in situations that cause you to use them.

Gratitude

How grateful are you? Do you remember to count your blessings every day? They are a lot, and we miss them because we dwell on the negative. Gratitude brings you to a happy place as you appreciate what you have. You can start by writing down events around you. A gratitude list affects your vibration frequency and mood. There is more to be grateful for, and doing so allows positive energy to flow into your life.

It is crucial to stay tuned to the right frequency, especially during these trying times. People are still reeling from the effects of the pandemic, and having the correct vibrational frequency can help us fight diseases, boost our immune system, and protect ourselves from external influences. Vibrational frequencies and their application in human health offer immense therapeutic benefits. While it helps to relieve us of pains and aches, it also keeps our mind, body, soul, and spirit in tune with higher forces and healthy.

We are powerful. Humans are powerful, and so are you. Whatever the challenge is, whether a health condition or a physical, mental or emotional problem, a positive outlook is the best healing option. Our attitude can make a big impact to how we feel, see, and perceive a situation and the surroundings. One study indicates that staying strong in the face of a severe or terminal condition can help you over- come it.

However, it is not magic; it is the power of positive thinking and aligning those thoughts with your vibrational energy. Simple daily affirmation or journaling your thoughts can quench the onset of mental issues like anxiety, depression and alter your outlook on life.

Everything is energy and Energy is everything. If you wish to understand the Universe, think of energy, frequency and vibration.

— NIKOLA TESLA

ALTERNATIVE MEDICINE

*N*atural healing has traditionally been regarded as a slow, often ineffective alternative to western medicine. This is not the case. In fact, many alternative healing technologies are far more advanced than what medical science offers. Quantum healing is often referred to as a "pseudo- science." This does not mean it is not legitimate or effective. It means that its effectiveness has not been proven by conventional western medicine standards. (Another way of saying this is that it still needs to be understood.)

Considering that fifty years ago, the idea of having a touch screen mobile phone that fits into the palm of your hand, with the ability to connect people face to face, do virtual banking and turn on your dish-washer from the office was the stuff of science fiction. Look back even ten or twenty years, and you will be amazed at the advances of technology in all domains.

The information I share about the power of quantum healing and the many cutting-edge alternative health technologies and modalities will be new for many of you. There are things we take for granted today that we might have scoffed at decades ago. But as the saying goes, "we don't know what we don't know."

Healing a Life Force Energy Imbalance

We all have the healing power tucked away deep within us. When we allow the body to release its energy and sort through it, we can return to the initial point of harmony. The ability to heal ourselves is a reality, and mastering it comes with absolute focus and understanding that you can.

Over the centuries, numerous worldwide restoration techniques from cultures, people, and communities have been readily available. Aside from deep approaches like chakra healing, Reiki, meditation, yoga, massage, acupuncture, or having a perfect laugh are ways to eliminate bad energy and restore harmony.

I learned each with ease and quickly moved into more uncommon, underground techniques, technologies and modalities. What surprised me was that these were not new, but proven and successful in getting people well. No matter what condition or how terminal, people were getting healed. However, I also saw how once Big Pharma and our government came to know and get involved, they disappeared into thin air.

Reiki

Reiki is an alternative healing therapy named after the Japanese theologist Dr. Mikao Usui. It is a natural healing method centered on the universal life force energy. Reiki is not a selective treatment for illnesses or a particular body part, as it believes that sickness will eventually spread throughout the body. When one undergoes Reiki, they meet with the reiki master, the vessel that receives the energy and then passes it onto the person desiring to heal. People who indulge in Reiki are livelier, more joyful, and more fulfilled as their energy level is enhanced. Additionally, Reiki protects the skin, body organs, and immune system.

During a Reiki treatment, the reiki master starts the process from the top of the head and works their way to the rest of the body, gradually dealing with stagnant energy and increasing seamless flow.

Chakra Healing

In chakra healing, the aura is a process of restoring energy balance. In the chakra-clearing method, the body consists of seven energy centers situated along the spine, known as the spiritual center. These centers are where imbalances start in the body depending on what is wrong with you; restoration creates energy balances at each point.

Aside from the above, there are more options as you continue reading, and we need to understand that these methods are safer than many orthodox treatments we choose.

Brain Optimization

A good friend of mine, Mariel Hemingway, the grand-daughter of Ernest Hemingway, reached out to me and wanted me to look into brain optimization, also known as neurofeedback. Thanks to her, I was trained, certified and licensed. I was able to help her from falling into the patterns that led her family into suicide, addiction and abuse. It greatly helped her, her family, friends and associates.

Brain Optimization is a way to create an acoustic mirror for the brain to see itself. Just as the brain see's a cut on your arm, it heals it. The brain will naturally heal itself from the inside out, creating new neuropathways and brining balance back to the brain. When the brain experiences stress or trauma it can get into stuck states. These stuck patterns are one of two survival states, freeze mode and fight or flight. When the brain is balanced, symptoms drop away. The brain doesn't know of labels that the doctors give us, so once the symptoms are gone, so is the label. I never cared to even ask or know what the issue was with my earlier clients unless they wanted me to know. Otherwise, I would hook them up to sensors that read their brain and showed me where to mirror the brain back to itself.

So many people would randomly say it healed their issue and other issues too! This is because the brain doesn't discriminate, it will address everything it finds to be out of balance and heal it. For instance, a lady with Lupus and IBS later told me she was a raging alcoholic. She admitted to drinking 2 bottles a night and now she may or may not have 2 glasses the whole week.

A famous baseball player was referred to me for his addiction of opiates. Money was no issue for him. He spent millions every year to try to solve his problem of addiction. When we met, I told him as long as I could show up 2-3 times a week to run the neurofeedback on him, his brain would do the rest. I knew that if he could quit or reduce, he would. I didn't even make that a requirement for our treatment plan. I explained to him that it was only a matter of time (1-3 months) before his brain was balanced and his decisions, behavior and motivation would change entirely. Sure enough, he called me 3 months later and told me he had pills in his hand and didn't know what to do with them. His pain was gone and his life felt better without them. With some new routines he quickly celebrated a full recovery. This was after millions were spend on treatments that didn't work. I used this technology for everything and it really worked well.

People flew from around the world to meet me, and in some cases I was flown to them. It didn't matter the age or condition, the brain (as the master control center of us), was a powerful, natural, non-invasive treatment. I have thousands of testimonials for just about everything ranging from Alopecia, Alzheimer's, Suicide, Addiction and more. People were leaving hospice, the hospital, years of being bedridden, paralyzed, in pain and more. It was very fulfilling and satisfying.

Light Therapy

Then along came a client where he had fallen from a lift inside Home Depot. His head was the size of a lampshade. I couldn't do the brain work on him until I knew I addressed the inflammation from his concussion. That is when I discovered infrared light therapy. This is an excellent way to reduce pain and inflammation while creating nitric oxide in the cells for rapid healing. This was a game changer for me because now I could work the brain and body and earn double for the same time.

Bio Resonance Scan

Our Bio Resonance Scanner was introduced after an 8 year old boy was brought to me. His parents were being pushed to get him on medication for ADHD. I was eager to help them; after all I was not a fan for medications, especially in children. Shocked, I didn't see any imbalance in his brain. I reached out to my global network of healers, doctors, scientists, and researches and was led to a Russian researcher and scientist. He showed me a demo of this technology. I was in such a hurry; I didn't have my DNA sent to him. He asked me to text a photo of myself, I did and within 5 minutes, the scan was reading me so accurately I jumped at the chance to get this technology so I could help this young boy. He seemed be crawling out of his skin, while getting kicked out of school and losing his friends. The discovery to the root cause for him was astounding. Little did I know the enormous impact this would make on thousands of people to follow. Parasites infested his brain and were the leading cause for his issue. After brining myself to have the courage of telling his parents, we used frequency healing to kill them without harming his brain or body. No medications or surgery was used. In less than 30 days he returned to the sweet boy he used to be.

This scanner had been used by NASA and in Russian space projects to detect health issues and heal astronauts in space. Its ability to read from DNA and report on top pathogens weakening the body was remarkable. It's so advanced we can prevent and turn around a person's health in a matter of days regardless of age, condition or location.

This device and software that we use to create test results can best be described as a quantum computer whose operations can harness the phenomena of quantum mechanics, such as superposition, interference, and entanglement.

On the testing device computer, a custom software program runs spinning electrons clockwise and counterclockwise inside of the device. The device then creates a torus vortex or toroidal energetic field around the sample, capturing its unique energetic properties. At the center of this field is called the zero point, where the quantum field and quantum information is accessible.

By sending a quantum information request into this field, our device will compute the highest probability of accurate bioenergetics measurements based on the database we are testing. The response will be a series of measurements to the given state of the client.

The technology is based on the premise that every cell, tissue, and organ has its own electromagnetic frequency or vibration, which changes according to your health condition at any given time. It takes measurements of your body's electrical, magnetic and energy fields in order to create a complete picture of your health.

Frequency Healing

Sound healing is not a new phenomenon; it has existed for ages, and one inventor who has made an immense contribution to the well-being of the human body and sound healing is Nikola Tesla. Perhaps, in what we would call a mistaken invention, Tesla discovered the power of sound healing via his oscillation machine. This simple device would later treat all types of health issues, from simple stomach pain to mental disorders, hormonal imbalances, and cardiovascular ailments.

But he was not the first and certainly not the last, as there are plenty returning to their roots and reviving the act of using sound and vibrations for healing.

Can you imagine having your cancer cells wiped out without surgery or pain? Can you imagine it costing under $5,000 dollars to reverse the diagnosis from "terminal cancer" to "cancer free"?

Many people have been told by their oncologist, "There's nothing more we can do for you, get your affairs in order"... but then through some means have learned that there *is hope. At first, it may seem unbelievable and even scary to try one more thing after battling through the conventional cancer treatment route...*

But many who have tried Dr. Royal Rife's Rife Frequency machine discovered that the pain was the first to go. If you're like many people, you've prob- ably never heard of Rife Frequency or its inventor, Dr. Royal Rife. But it's a story worth learning – especially for anyone touched by cancer.

Who Was Dr. Royal Rife?

Dr. Royal Rife (1888-1971) was an incredibly intelligent microbiologist with a passion for healing. Dr. Royal Rife' was willing to sacrifice everything to save humanity from suffering from terminal cancer.

The medical mafia has done much to destroy these devices and the men that developed them over the last 110 years. But fortunately, there *are* good people who keep working for our benefit. And in keeping with The Truth About Cancer's message of hope. It is my intention here to bring hope to those suffering that it IS possible to conquer cancer. We see it every day!

In the early 1900s, Dr. Royal Rife built the Universal Microscope. Because of this tool, Dr. Royal Rife was awarded the honor of being the first to discover, by viewing it live, the cancer virus that attacks human cells.

Dr. Royal Rife discovered the unique spectroscopic signature of each cancer virus. Then Dr. Royal Rife used the color wavelength (spectroscopic signature) to make them visible under the virus microscope (Universal Microscope).

The science behind this is the resonant frequency in light wavelengths. The individual beam or light ray hits the virus and the virus resonates or vibrates making it visible under the special microscope. Similar to sound waves, we hear the sound a certain way because of the vibration it makes in our ears. The sound can also be felt as a vibration, which is the way people who are deaf can detect sound. This resonance is significant because it matches each type of cancer virus uniquely.

What Is the RIFE Frequency?

After several years of tracking these cancer virus, Dr. Royal Rife developed a technique referred to as the RIFE Frequency. Simply put, he used the resonant frequency (the frequency that the virus vibrates at) to cause the virus to oscillate and then turned up the intensity or volume if you will. This resulted in the structural integrity of the virus collapsing and destroying itself.

The good news is, every cell and bacteria resonate at their own unique frequency with healthy cells vibrating at a higher frequency. As a result, only the targeted cancer virus gets destroyed, without damage to the person.

Dr. Royal Rife Tests His Experimental Treatment

In 1934, Dr. Royal Rife was given a number of human test subjects, who were essentially left to die because no more could be done for them by the cancer industry. After Rife's Treatments, 86.5% of the patients were completely cancer free, 13.5% received an adjusted treatment (more potent) for an additional 30 days and then they also became 100% cancer-free.

In conclusion, his technology was 100% effective against terminal (stage IV) cancer in all of the participants.

Not Everyone Wants a Cure for Cancer

Just like today, not everyone is excited about this success. Dr. Royal Rife's technology posed a huge threat to the cancer industry and medical institutions in general who, according to statistics, get most of their revenue from oncology. In other words, if cancer can be cured they would go bankrupt – and lose out on making billions of dollars treating cancer patients.

Similar to today, the cancer industry was dedicated to preventing the public from discovering that there was a painless treatment that had a 100% cure rate for terminal cancer. It was also inexpensive because it operated on a minimal amount of electricity.

The medical establishment didn't want people to get the "dangerous idea" that they didn't need drugs; that would mean they didn't need Big Pharma!

The medical mafia (American Medical Association, American Cancer Society, and FDA) was on the trail to stamp out, obliterate, and debunk the truth before it could ever get out. And they were pretty successful... for a while, until they destroyed his reputation, threatened anyone who knew him and then killed him, making it look like a suicide. (A common theme even today.)

Bottom line, science understands the power of the metaphysical and that, at certain frequencies; one can repel negative energy, including diseases. We cannot ignore the link between health, healing, well-being, and vibrations. According to quantum physics, the universe is a compendium of energies. We live in this energy bubble, and according to our alignment, we attract the best or worst toward us.

Remember, our actions also have the power to alter what we receive. Science acknowledges that each human cell or organ has a particular sonic signature; this means that when exposed to a certain vibrational frequency, your skin cells will react and your heart cells will not. For example, when body parts are diseased, it means they are not producing the accurate vibrational frequency or they are out of tune. Therefore, to restore these cells or organs to optimal function, we must create a frequency that eliminates the pain and restores their function.

Everything affects our vibrational frequency, even unresolved and traumatic experiences, because we store them in our organs, thereby declining their optimal vibrational frequency levels and well-being.

Ideally, human beings operate on a high vibrational frequency level to enjoy good health and wellness. So to ensure you are always "alive," below are seven things that can affect you.

Quantum physics acknowledges two vibrational energies: positive and negative. Any of them can alter how you feel at any point.

Frequency Healing is was and still is a leading therapy. Because we are just energy, using energy to change energy was very effective. We call that inside out healing. Outside-in healing such as taking supplements were not as effective. The capabilities were endless and so were the successful healing stories.

These and other modalities came into play such
as ozone therapy, energy shifting, sound healing
and more.

15

COVID & THE VACCINATION

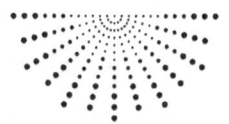

COVID-19 & The VAX

When the world was on lockdown, my first goal was to figure out how to support our clients remotely. Fortunately, we were able to accomplish this using many of our existing advanced technologies. Our licensed practitioners sent programmable brain headsets to those suffering from anxiety, depression, and suicidal ideation, which are monitored just as though they are in our office. We used our bio-resonance scanner to test and facilitate remote healing of the physical body through frequencies.

This accesses energy in the quantum field. We were able to help hundreds of clients facing death in the ICU with no physical contact. We conducted hundreds of scans through clients photos and DNA. There will be more about this in Chapter 18.

As the world continues to experience the COVID-19 virus spread, it has become apparent that there have been lapses due to the "infodemic" and reported deaths among vaccinated individuals. While many still refer to COVID-19 and the vaccine as "flu," and individuals must get vaccinated according to the latest strain, it is clear that there is no strategy to curb the virus, and we all have to live with it for a long time.

Conspiracy theories attempt to explain the cause of an event like the pandemic with claims of plots by elite figures. That is what happened with the pandemic. Some say it came from a lab in China, and then we heard it was produced under lab conditions but somehow got out of hand, and the whole world is suffering from the mistake or intentionality of a group of people.

This is the chapter you may have a hard time accepting. It was also the hardest to write. There is so much more information to share, which will come in the next book edition. I could keep quiet about this, but I have a moral obligation to share my experience and fact-based evidence with the world, or at least with those who will listen with an open mind. There is no benefit to me, no agenda. You do not have to believe me. Remember, knowledge is power, and if you look, you will find plenty of evidence of the truth from your own research. Look beyond mainstream media because they are all controlled on what to say and not say. Go to free speech sites such as Rumble, TruthSocial, Telegram, Children's Health Defense, Epoch Times, etc.

Do your research, but remember that you cannot rely on mainstream media or even Facebook and Google. The truth is being suppressed and controlled.

The Vaccine Mis-Truth

During COVID-19, especially after the vaccines came out, our clients' bio-scans started to show the craziest things. It was detecting things like snake venom, Myocarditis, cancer, and HIV! I was so baffled when these things showed up on our clients scan reports that I began to think our technology was misreading. Why and how is it detecting the same thing for every client? I didn't

know what to make of it until two events oc-
curred. The first one was a family of five. They
came in, and they all showed the same thing. The
parents were older, and I thought there was no
way they had HIV, cancer, snake venom, and Myocarditis along with their three kids! The only
common theme was the vaccination.

Secondly, I happened to scan my own daughter,
who lives across the country from me, and she
showed it as well. I had no idea she got vaccinated. She couldn't be vaccinated, I thought. She
was always against them. After questioning her,
she explained she felt trapped and could not go
anywhere without it, such as the grocery stores,
public transportation, etc.

There is no judgment here to her or anyone for
that matter. But remember my Chapter Fear Will
Kill You? My best quality is that I never judge
people. Nobody should judge others, as we are
not in others' shoes. Millions of people, including
my own family members were scared, frightened
and driven to take measures that, if not addressed, will be catastrophic to their health.

I did not disclose to her what I saw, to not create
fear. I just focused on reversing the problem. I

quickly detoxed her through some natural remedies and used our remote meta-therapies using frequency healing. It took six months and continued monitoring.

I would not have written this book without my personal experience witnessing these facts and evidence. I was not even privy to the rumors and conspiracy theories surrounding COVID-19 and the vaccine until my own experience, working with hundreds of clients prompted me to double-check and question even minor discrepancies.

Our technology showed that the vaccine not only harms people, but alters human DNA. As outrageous as it sounds, the test results from scans of vaccinated people prove that something is not right.

Many people witnessed the vaccine to cause health complications, particularly in obese, elderly or those with a predisposition in their health, unknown or known. Even babies and children who were previously healthy and full of life before receiving the shot are facing major health issues as well as death. One birthing facility reported that nine out of ten newborn babies are being born as still births.

The whole thing does not make sense, but you decide. During the pandemic, social media was tightly regulated and controlled. Nobody could share solutions to the masses, including me. We were permanently banned! This further discredited the efficacy of the vaccine and exposes the true agenda at hand.

The COVID-19 and De-Population Agenda

Not all COVID-19 vaccinations are the same; otherwise, the agenda of depopulation would be too obvious. I did get total confirmation that our technology was not broken and was indeed reading accurately. So again, we have an advantage. I have proof beyond thousands of hospitals, doctors, and clinics. This is not hearsay; this is the black-and-white truth from actual experience!

COVID-19 was not just another virus; it was a biological instrument fabricated to manipulate the human mind by a few global elites as a mode to control, reduce, divide, rule, and influence an agenda of global governance. As mentioned, the virus was engineered and distributed to several laboratories worldwide as a bioweapon called the vaccine. Consider the well-known pharmaceutical company Moderna. Whether you believe it or not, it was a startup by the US Defense Advanced Research Project Agency to turn gene therapies into mRNA vaccines.

I am not degrading the success of global immunization over the years, especially in saving millions, keeping life-threatening diseases at bay, and giving people a lease on living longer and healthier. Those took decades of testing and proven results. The pandemic reminded the world of the power of vaccines to save lives, and even though many died, it was part of the process until a potent and efficient vaccine was manufactured. However, attached to the COVID-19 vaccine is the 2030 agenda. This is a depopulation agenda, many would have heard billionaire Bill Gates and Charles Schwab discuss it; how the human population is reaching levels that the planet cannot sustain. The immunization agenda 2030 was supposedly a strategy by the World Health Assembly and its partners in several countries to address over- population changes and eventually manage them.

The damage is already done, and the draconian laws implemented during the lockdown are still affecting many today. I know this may be hard to hear and scary, but again, there is nothing to fear because there are solutions to everything. There are actually hundreds of doctors who know about this agenda. Like me, they are helping to provide solutions to help people with the vaccination injury. There are thousands of injured people from around the world, and even more who died suddenly.

The truth is being brought to light about the motives and greed behind it. The necessary changes will occur, but we must wake up and speak up. I have a moral duty to share my experience and knowledge. What I saw in vaccinated people's scans led me to further truth and awareness.

It's despicable to watch people profit over people's suffering. The World Health Organization is on a global strategic mission to carry out an agenda to depopulate the earth down to 500 million. Claims about global warming are the basis for this. They believe they can have more control by creating part-human, part-computer transgenderism. The elites plan rid the world of the people they cannot control and create humans who can be controlled.

In September, Senator Rand Paul asked Dr. Fauci to divulge information concerning COVID-19 and who is or is not benefiting from it, which he clearly did not get an answer to. So if you are sitting back in your home thinking it is okay to continually get boosters, then I am sorry to surprise you, as many more will be coming. It is crazy, yet no one seems to understand the gravity of the vaccine and the long-term impact of the pandemic.

Don't you see that we are playing right into the hands of the global elite? The agenda is to create division among us, causing us to lose our spiritual connection and connection with each other as humans. They are dumbing us down through social media and 5G frequencies, causing confusion, fear, while distracting us through the mainstream media with BLM & the threat of nuclear war. They are slowing poisoning us internally and externally while injecting people with the COVID-19 vaccination, which is actually a bioweapon! Spiked proteins found in the blood are venom peptides. Venom reduces oxygen in the blood which cause death through a variety of ways.

Myocarditis shows a 25% fatality rate for people in the first 2 years and a rate of 50% in the next 5 years. This includes children and teens! How is it not outrageous to hear of "sudden adult death" or heart attacks in children now? Google "died suddenly"! It was and still is the number one searched word globally. Watch the documentary Died Suddenly.

Ultimately the global elites are reducing our financial system, food supply, creating confusion, scarcity, and fear so that we fold and conform or die.

It is predicted that people will die of unknown causes anywhere between 3 months and 6 years due to an increase in liver, viral, parasitic, and brain diseases; cardiac issues; strokes; and an overall increase in all diseases. Watch the documentary "Died Suddenly," which became a top-searched word on the internet. SIDS was a common cause of infant death. Now we are seeing adult sudden deaths and heart attacks in children. Come on!

Really, you don't see what is happening here? We have to wake up and be conscious of what is taking place. Have you heard the story of the frog placed in a pot of water? The water was slowly heated up without the frog knowing, until it was too late. The frog didn't realize what was happening, so it never bothered trying to escape and died. Don't let this be you.

VAERS Report

VAERS is an authorized body of the US Food and Drug Administration that monitors the safety of vaccines. Additionally, it ensures that any vaccine distributed in the US is safe, but how effective was it during the pandemic? Less than 1% was reported to VAERS prior to the pandemic. The CDC refused Harvard's help to improve it and make it more accurate. Due to the under reporting, it is estimated the COVID-19 vaccine caused over 3 million unreported deaths. Let's look at what it says:

- https:// vaccineimpact.com/ 2022/government- vaers-data-reveal-15600-increase-in- heart-disease-among= under-30-year- olds-following-covid-19-vaccination/
- Vaccine Impact - Government VAERS Data Reveal:

- 15,600% Increase in Heart Disease Among Under 30 Year-Olds Following COVID-19
- Vaccination - Vaccine Impact The U.S. Government's Vaccine Adverse Events Reporting System (VAERS) released more data into the database maintained by the CDC and FDA today, and there are now 1,071,856 reports of deaths.

This is just the tip of the iceberg. I urge you to conduct your own research, we cannot show a blind eye to what is openly going on in the world. The questions are numerous, but the answers come in trickles. It is time for us as humans to heal ourselves and take control back into our own hands.

We have believed lies for so long, and unlearning what we have learned is going to be a challenge. And I understand that, but what exactly is stopping you from trying alternative healing methods or even bringing your body to a state of self-healing?

With decades in the healing field, I know the power we have within. Sometimes you need someone to push you forward in your healing journey.

COVID-19 Vaccine Impacts the Immune System

Each time you are injected, you are decreasing your immune system. You are putting your life at risk. The predicted survival rate for those vaccinated and boosted is 3 to 5 years. If you do something about it then this doesn't have to be true for you.

Our wellness center is being flooded with desperate clients facing everything from erratic ovulation cycles to neurological issues to heart arrhythmias. There is a 6,000 percent increase in cancers, cardiovascular issues, and unexplained deaths. I know we are not the only ones seeing this. Some are in on it, others are under the control of their higher ups while others are simply clueless.

Some countries around the world such as New Zealand are forcing their citizens, (including newborns) to take the 2nd, 3rd, and even 4th doses of the COVID-19 booster, which triggers the body to produce more antibodies against the virus. While that is what traditional vaccines should do. However, this is not what we think it is.

Spike Protein

Blood clotting has been associated with COVID-19 and the vaccine, and spike protein is the culprit. The heart is getting inflamed, which promotes a lack of blood flow in the heart.

Some reports have shown that the S-protein can disrupt the blood-brain barrier and damage endothelial cells with its side effects. They include chills, appetite loss, nausea, fever, joint and muscle aches, swollen lymph glands, and many other passive symptoms. These can also be associated with oxidative stress, which tires the body and makes you more susceptible to illness.

The COVID-19 deaths associated with blood clots are another baffling aspect of this VAX injury that is alarming. Several studies conducted by researchers in the United Kingdom and Sweden have linked blood clots to life-threatening conditions such as pulmonary embolism, heart attacks, paralysis, and strokes. While doctors are not connecting these deaths with the vaccination, coroners are seeing a connection as they speak up about the clotting of blood found in the bodies of dead children, athletes, and men and women of all ages.

The Great Awakening is a term you may have heard used to awaken people to what is happening right before our eyes!

People endure suffering and trauma until they realize the truth.

View the documentary Died Suddenly.

You can't make this up!

SOLUTIONS:

Many solutions range from frequency healing with Rife Technology to natural supplements. The bottom line is to take action for yourself and your loved ones. You have been warned. It is time to take action with a thorough cleansing of your body systems.

The process to reverse the effects of the jab will vary person to person but in general will look as follows:

- 90-day detox
- 90-day recovery

- 90-day regeneration

STEP ONE: Get Tested.

It is good to know what is going on and have a baseline to know if you are getting better or worse. Request a D-diver test, called a thrombolytic, through your doctor, which is a blood clotting test. Or ideally, get tested using a bio-resonance scanner like the one we use. It will give the earliest warning signs as an excellent preventative. We are already testing people of all ages who are experiencing unusual heart sensations such as arrhythmia, pain or fatigue. A bio-resonance scan, which scans on an energetic level are very accurate and sensitive, catching issues early on. These systems are more common in other countries and are considered "underground" in the United States.

STEP TWO: Boost the Immune System.

Vitamins A, D, E, and K2 are building blocks for the immune system. Our immune system is supported by three organs: bone marrow, thymus, and spleen. Keep your immune system boosted with selenium (200 mg), 1000–5000 mg of vitamin C, and 20 mg of zinc.

Natural immunity will always be better than artificial immunity (such as injections). Eat well, live well, and think well. Healing from disease is not difficult. I know this might have just pissed you off, but let's be real. If you had the right information and tools to put your body in a state of recovery, you would recover, or better yet, prevent yourself from getting sick! Many times, the disease is a buildup of emotions that forces you to go through pain. Start paying attention to your body and the signs. Only you will heal yourself.

Getting fresh air is a critical component of good health and the treatment of any illness, particularly COVID-19. This is why wearing a mask and staying indoors should be a dead giveaway that you are being misled. The CDC announced long ago that the masks do not stop the spread of the virus. Masks also prevent the inhalation of oxygen, which is an essential component of life force energy!

Getting direct sunlight without sunscreen, for 10– 20 minutes twice a day is a great source of vitamin D. Studies makes it clear that low vitamin D is a risk factor for getting COVID-19 and having a worse outcome and a higher risk of dying. Vitamin D3 in oil in capsules is better absorbed than tablets and is an excellent source of supplemental vitamin D if you cannot be outside in the sunshine, or if your blood level of vitamin D is too low. We will describe in upcoming chapters more about doses, how to check your blood levels of vitamin D, and other helpful laboratory studies.

Drink plenty of fluids—preferably distilled water, not beverages with sugars and additives. This is fundamental to keeping your immune system working well and keeping your body healthier to fight off the virus. Adequate hydration is crucial, and the amount will vary by body weight, but a good rule of thumb is that your urine should be the color of pale straw. If your urine is dark yellow or gold, you are definitely not drinking enough water. If your urine is colorless, you are drinking too much plain water, and this can make you feel lightheaded or confused from an electrolyte imbalance.

A healthy diet provides your body with the nutrients it requires to function well. Fresh, organic fruits and vegetables are good choices, along with healthy proteins. Avoid excess sugar and excessive intake of "convenience" foods high in fat, sugar, salt, and additives because these foods cause inflammation and weaken the immune system. Take immune-boosting vitamins and minerals: vitamin D, vitamin C, and zinc.

Fevers

Keep in mind that a fever is one of the body's defenses against infection and a sign of a potentially serious infection. Since fever may indicate a super- infection that requires aggressive antibiotic treatment rather than just medicine to lower the temperature, not all doctors agree that every fever should be treated. Acetaminophen, ibuprofen, and/or ice packs can be used to treat a high fever. Ice packs are a good option for reducing fever and are simple to use.

Fill a bag with ice and apply it to your back, stomach, or flanks. Oxidative stress on the liver is one of the side effects of acetaminophen. It may increase the risk of oxygen desaturation, according to one study. Alternating between ibuprofen and acetaminophen every four to six hours is one option. For instance, if the fever continues, administer ibuprofen at 12 p.m., followed by acetaminophen at 6 p.m. Try not to surpass the suggested portions on the pack.

STEP THREE: Detox

This stops the decline but also allows you to review other medications and their effects in addressing your conditions. For your body to enjoy this process, we advise all our clients, whether in-house or virtual, to carry out a body and cell detox. This removes all toxin build-up from major organs like the liver and kidneys, and this rejuvenation also helps cells attain a better functioning status. Detoxification must be diligently followed.

It is very important to detox and heal the liver. Now we have more through the vaccination. Spider and snake venom, showing in vaccinated can stay in the body for 10 years.

Ivermectin stopped COVID-19 because it binds to nicotine receptors in the brain stem. You can start slowly by using nicotine patches or 2 ml of gum. Ivermectin stops the venom. COVID-19 affected less than 2% of nicotine smokers. Ivermectin (1-2 times per week) and hydroxychloroquine are very effective medications, but most people are unaware of them or dismiss them. Over 20 million people heard about it on Rumble, and it saved hundreds of lives. Ivermectin protects venom from nerve damage.

There are a number of things that have been proven to be helpful. The key is detoxifying from the harmful jab. Research some or all of these and see what is right for you.

Supplements List:

- Chlorine Dioxide or MMS (read more by Andreas Kalcker), proven to heal thousands of conditions with no adverse effects. https://drive.google.com/file/d/1ecTbPAt6AIOht7e6cZe19XpsuXXZxtnu/view?usp=share_link
- Ivermectin paste/gel 2x daily, hydroxychloroquine
- Quercetin 250 mg
- Probiotic 3 caps 3x daily
- Zinc (plant-based organic zinc) 7 ml grams twice a dayDistilled water (takes out chemicals in your system)
- CDP-Choline
- Nano-kinase (dissolves pre-existing clots) Insulin into the nasal cavity: chronic neurological diseases
- Vitamin C and hydrocortisone (adrenal deficiency)

- 500 ml of NAC reduces clotting
- For tinnitus, loss of taste, and vertigo, neurological issues detox with Bentonite clay. Consume omega-3 fatty acids (3000K), which repair taste, smell, and memory loss.
- Urine (proven over 5K years)
- Glutathione
- NAC
- EDTA
- 200 mg /day of Selenium instructs the liver to produce glutathione and protect cells

Respiratory:

- 1.2 oz of 3% food grade hydrogen peroxide, colloidal silver, 1 drop DMSO and fill rest with distilled water. Shake and fill nebulizer (9 breaths in nose)

Technologies / Modalities

- Urine Therapy (drinking, enema, bathing, applying on skin, in belly button, aged urine) 3-6 oz midstream urine
- Frequency Healing using Rife Technology

- Cold therapy (11mins a week 0-6 Celsius)
- Hydro-therapathy
- Ozone therapy (neutralizes pathogens)
- Ultralight
- Hyperbaric chambers
- Detox Baths (2 cups kosher sea salt, 2 cups baking salt, 3-5 drops of DMSO, 1/8th teaspoon of borax/boron) soak and breath for a 1/2 hour. Skin is our biggest organ and considered the 3rd kidney. Look at your water with a black light after and see the toxins!

STEP FOUR: Regeneration Repair the DNA

At this stage, all clients should do a 3–5-day water fast. This is a general health recovery strategy that works from the inside out to heal the body. It allows the cells a rest period that enables them to cleanse and renew themselves for the workdays ahead.

Hunger is not a bad sign; it is your body telling you that it is working and needs fuel. Furthermore, if it has been genetically modified or damaged by the shot, this process will restore it and cause regeneration. It is a strict process, and you must be committed to going the entire nine yards, including juicing protocols, eating super-foods, and eliminating any artificial, GMO, biologically altered, or chemically added foods. Other recommendations are: intermittent fasting, cold plunges, breathing exercises, meditation, frequency healing, neurofeedback, and light therapy. These help in eliminating toxins in your external and internal environment, while eliminating unknown fears to reconnect us back to our spiritual and human selves.

• Frequency Healing using Rife and Tesla Technologies can help restore DNA

• MRNA alters our DNA. The only thing that remembers our DNA coding is our urine. The most powerful enzyme for preventing blood clots!Urine Therapy: **Urine contains your original coding of your DNA. (Read all about it in the next book. Your own perfect antidote: Urotherapy.com**

https://www.healthguidance.org/entry/15626/1/Health-Benefits-of-Urotherapy.html

• 3-5 day fasting has also proven to repair DNA

SHEDDING

If you did not receive the jab and are experiencing symptoms, you are suffering from shedding. I personally have to detox myself as I am exposing myself daily to the vexed. COVID-19 and/or vaccinations are transmitted through shedding. I personally have been exposed to over 3000 COVID Positive & vaccine-exposed clients. I didn't wear a mask, and I didn't get the jab. All I did was keep my immune system strong.

Stay away from 5G towers and try to detox and repair DNA damage. If you took the jab, then it is critical to detox the poison (heavy metals, parasites, and venom). Spike proteins cause issues to be magnified with carbs and sugars, so those must be reduced and limited.

Treating COVID-19 (or the next pandemic) at Home

We have found that treating COVID-19 clients at home quickly, when symptoms develop, led to better outcomes and dramatically lower death rates.

Medical clinic care for primary patients has a much higher mortality rate and a much higher risk of long-term lung, heart, neurological, and other complications for those who survive. Another reason why home-based treatment makes sense is that it lessens the spread of the illness. The COVID-19 virus is highly contagious. In addition to evaluating patients' symptoms and vital signs (which can be taken at home), we now have a safer option for remote patient evaluation through telemedicine.

Thanks to modern technology, we no longer require ill patients to visit the office in person and run the risk of infecting others.

Home care is safer because it reduces the risk of picking up other infections from sick people in the hospital. The healthcare system in most countries worldwide is different from what we see in the USA. In the US, patients that come in sick are usually asked to go home until their case worsens, which is why the COVID-19 pandemic was so high.

If sick patients were immediately isolated and treated, perhaps it would be easier for doctors or medical practitioners to handle the problem. It will also help limit the spread while monitoring any adverse vaccine reactions.

Home care also allows people to have family members with them for love and support. It can be terrifying to be seriously ill in the hospital, and it's even worse to have family unable to visit. Even though nurses are trained to care for and cater to patients, having your loved ones around you aids in healing. They are your support system, and many hospitalized victims lacked access to this love and died alone as the medical team was overwhelmed and exhausted.

Home care can quickly use widely available, low-cost generic oral medicines and help avoid the risks of IV medicines needed when people are critically ill in the hospital. Physicians can prescribe home-based oxygen therapy with oxygen concentrators available through home health services. Oxygen concentrators can be purchased without a prescription online or for cash from some local suppliers for as little as a few hundred dollars.

All the treatment modalities used in hospitals, except for mechanical ventilators, can be implemented at home faster and more effectively, and they are better tailored to the individual patient.

Even the best vaccines for flu are only about 30–60% effective. Compare that to the efficacy for improvement ranging from 64% to more than

90% in over 100 new studies demonstrating early, outpatient treatment for COVID-19 with our existing medications described in the chapters. Delayed side effects (e.g., infertility, cancer, and autoimmune diseases) may not be seen for years.

Blood clots, Guillain-Barré syndrome, Myocarditis, and Pericarditis have already prompted FDA warnings. These may be mild or rare, but vigilance is required to provide early treatment. Monitoring should be done on D-dimers and other blood coagulation tests. An educational resource from the Association of American Physicians and Surgeons (AAPSonline.org) states on page 24 that mild weak- ness sometimes progresses rapidly to respiratory paralysis requiring mechanical ventilation. An MRI, ultrasound, or blood troponin levels—an enzyme released when heart cells are damaged—help to diagnose heart inflammation. Be aware of potential dangers!

There are thousands of people reaching out due to post-vaccination symptoms. If that is you, know that you are not alone. These experimental shots are affecting many people.

If you are having issues post-COVID-19 or the vaccination, then these are some natural remedies for your chronic fatigue, loss of taste and smell, tinnitus, heart arrhythmia, brain, heart, intestinal, histamine, kidney, and water retention.

Remember, every disease can be healed and eliminated! People do not always want to be healed. Are you willing to do what it takes?

Hope and Belief

Our mind is a powerful platform that can both grow and destroy. Yes, healing starts in the mind. When we accept and agree that we can heal, then healing can happen. Self healing our bodies can heal them- selves from any traumatic experience, including COVID-19. You cannot deny that the pandemic shook the foundation of our existence and dissolved everything we thought we knew about science, medicine, or the government. However, you can heal completely from all the pain associated with COVID-19, irrespective of the damage. If you make it, you can heal and renew your cells too.

We are in tune with a higher force, and when we align our inner energy with it, we can control our healing abilities. If you have never self-healed before, now is a good time to reach out to me and get your healing mechanisms up and running.

Healing frequency is unique to every person. Some clients have described the experience as soothing, cold, relaxing, or warm, while others battle with their thoughts before finding a comfortable place.

Each client must come to a peaceful place before starting the 90-day detox, recovery, and regeneration journey. This can be done via breathing techniques, better sleep patterns, or meditation.

COVID-19 was a stressful era. People suffering from the disease or their loved ones were subjected to undue stress. This was not made easy with the strict lockdown rules that literally disconnected us from our Zen place. Our clients experienced a shift in feeling from uncertainty to mindfulness.

Everyone has a self-healing mechanism. People do not know how powerful and safe these remedies are. The human body is so complicated, with millions of microorganisms within us. There are more options to try. Some jump in 100%. Others will not. There is something for everyone, even those who cannot afford anything.

16

PREVENTION

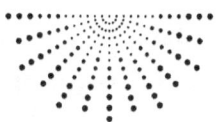

*I*f we took small steps in all areas of our lives to do good, be good and transfer good, our lives will be better.

THERE IS nothing to worry about if you keep your immune system strong. Sunlight, organic/non-gmo foods, rest, exercise, positive people, eliminate stressors and fears.

Today, we have many ways to prevent disease and illness. As mentioned in the beginning of this book, knowledge is the key the health. You are in charge of your health, so be educated and proactive about it.

One of the most exciting days of my practice was when we received our bio-resonance scanner, which reads energy. Because we are made up of energy, can read those frequencies and match it to those frequencies stored the energetic calculation of everything. DNA, genes, chromosomes, cells, nerves, bones, and organs are measured and evaluated on their end-energetic vibration.

Our Bio-resonance scanner can help show our past, present, and future health without harmful radiation to our bodies. Again, and sadly, this is something not common in the United States but more common in other countries. There is so much we can do to prevent disease and illness. Our bio resonance scanner can detect the first abnormal cell growth, whereas western technology takes 8 years and 32 million cancer cells later to be detected. It is regrettable.

We can see parasites anywhere, such as the brain and heart wall, wherein western technology can only detect them through urine, stool, or blood. Our advanced technology allows you to have non-invasive breast and prostate exams without clients even coming to our office. Does this sound too good to be true?

Doctors can't always verify what our scans detect. A Bio Resonance Scanner goes far beyond the technology of an MRI or CTC scan. It often takes a longer time to show up if at all. This makes prevention difficult.

I will never forget the look on everyone's face when I was sent in to help a woman who was told she was brain dead, or a vegetable. But when these clients were up and ready to return home in 2-4 weeks, the doctors would explain that they don't have access to the same technology as we do. That is a pretty honest answer.

Listen To Your Body.

Tune in and listen to your body. If you have yeast infections, yellow toe nails, itchy scalp, painful bowls, etc., this means your body is trying to tell you something. Something is not right! Don't ignore it. Get it checked out. Trust your gut, your intuition and face your fears. When we postpone simple things, we will eventually have to face them. But consider these checks through advanced holistic centers that are non-harmful and non-invasive and can see beyond CTC and MRI scans.

. . .

MOVE AND MOVE MORE.

We live in a lazy generation that wants the best of life without working for it. Technology gives us access to many luxuries, but our bodies remain strong by moving. I am not asking you to run a marathon; a simple walk around the neighborhood is fine. Remember to be consistent; that is how we see results.

Watch your Body Mass.

Many people need to learn their body mass or how to calculate their BMI. These are simple, free tools available everywhere and on your mobile device to check your weight and how close you are to being obese. If overweight or obese, you are at a higher risk of developing or triggering health issues like cancer and breathing problems. Your BMI should be a watchpoint that gears you towards a healthier path.

Stop Smoking.

If you smoke, you are prone to lung problems and breathing problems. If you do not smoke but are continually around smokers, you are also prone to diseases like strokes and heart problems.

. . .

Sleep/Rest/Nap

Sleep restores our mental, emotional, and physical strength. Additionally, you can avoid sugar and sugary foods, heavy foods, and alcohol before bed. If you have trouble sleeping, check with your doctor and develop a sleep routine that works for you.

Detox. Detox. Detox!

We need to detox from the outside and inside factors. We need to detox from the things we control and the things out of our control mentioned in the Chapter, Outside Factors. Nearly all conditions are pathogenic (meaning the underlying root cause are parasites, viruses, bacteria, fungus, EMFs, and heavy metals).

"An ounce of prevention is worth a pound of care."

17

A NEW MINDSET, A NEW YOU

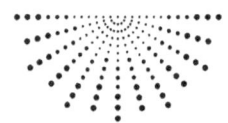

"The body heals with play, the mind heals with laughter, and the spirit heals with joy."

Throughout this book, we talked about energy, and when we decide to heal, we must open ourselves up to enable some things to leave us and good things to come into us. Alas, this is more challenging than saying it.

Often, clients who struggled for 20 years or more before healing through our advanced modalities become stuck in the identity of being labeled. They shut their hearts and minds, choosing to remain in that place of comfort even though it might not be most of the time. When we accept unusual or incorrect perceptions, they gradually become acceptable, and the aura picks them up and adopts them. Labeling is wrong. It depends on which side of the fence you are on, but it is time to step out and be different, a new kind of other. A set of symptoms define the label. Many labels make it easier for doctors to describe what you have.

But there is a much bigger issue to address here. The brain does not know of labels, and when doing neurofeedback and brain optimization, the brain becomes balanced, symptoms go away, and the tag goes away. We become conditioned by our doctors, family, and friends that we have this disease or illness and identify with it. We take that on like a new skin.

And this is why many people take ages to opt for another option in healing. I agree that words are powerful and capable of shifting our realities and creating another, but you have a mouth, too; start creating the truths you want to see. When some sick people come to see me, I always ask them why it took so long to search for answers. Why did they neglect their healing? I learned from their response that they are stuck in a label and believe they cannot heal or are afraid of being labeled again.

If a label makes you feel boxed in, it is time to shatter that closure, and it begins with your mind. It would help if you learned to stop analyzing the negative thoughts or allocating power to them. They only succeed in keeping you stagnated. It means you keep going down the same path, receiving the same results and anticipating the same feeling. Read the chapter on support groups. Whether searching for answers on healing or recovering, you need people who create a positive aura around you or see the best in terrible situations, including your label. Remember, the tag was identification. You can change it, but you must accept that you can first.

We are energy surrounded by energy, and what we emit is what we receive. I do not know how to simplify this deeply profound thought. The truth is, even when we heal, if we cannot step away from that label, we can kill the good energy that can help us transit to a full recovery. Every time you allow your mindset to return to a place of captivity, you try to define the label, and you want to listen to people address your past every time you are grounding your capability to create a new you and a new mindset.

It is perilous. It takes effort to undo the energy and end the identity that you have worn for so long. One of my clients, who had cancer for four years, no longer has cancer. However, she was petrified to share this great news with her family. She was also terrified about who she would be if she did not have cancer. The attention was friendly, the extra help was beautiful, and who would she be if she was not cancerous?

I told her to take baby steps and practice talking to strangers about how she is no longer a cancer victim. Eventually, she became more and more comfortable. What you talk about is what you attract. If you think you are, then you are. The mind is a powerful thing. You have heard of people curing themselves simply by focusing on each cell in their body, seeing it healthy again.

We hear miraculous stories about people using the power of the mind and positive thinking and visualization. I use the term "fake it till you make it." If someone is diagnosed with a disease or illness, I encourage them not to share it with others but rather take 30 days and get rid of it.

Steps to Creating a New Mindset, Creating a New You

Be Quiet, Be Calm and Relax

It is the first step to creating a new mindset and new you, your new self. Humans love being busy. In today's fast-paced world, it is easy to get lost and drowned in noise (primarily harmful), and being still is not a natural tendency we have. However, to win and erase every label, you must practice being still and quiet and visualize where you can be in your new self. Stop being selfish and trying to remain in your terrible past when you have the power to over- come it; it is not fair. It is time to keep quiet.

Power Begets Power

A new mindset will be difficult, especially for people trying to erase a painful past. However, by engaging in activities that build up your positive energy, like physical exercise (looking good makes anyone feel good), yoga, meditation, and communing with nature, you start to step into the new. Remember, your entire day can be as good as you desire or as mediocre as you want it to be. The choice is yours. So I tell my clients to remove anything that triggers a painful past from their lives.

"If you think you can or you think you can't, you are right."

- Henry Ford

When you are diagnosed with a chronic condition, cancer, or terminal ailment, it is understandable when fear, anger, sadness, and pain are the only emotions you see and feel. Dwelling on the negative and being ungrateful can keep you limited. Focus on what is right not what is not right. After the recovery or during the healing process, it is para- mount to note grateful acts along the way. Grateful- ness speeds the healing process, eliminates negative vibrational energies, and aligns us with powers that allow our brains to rethink the old into something new. I encourage people to create a "be grateful journal." This notepad is to jot down the good parts as you recover complete control of your life, sickness free. Unlike most people, I encourage people to be grateful for what they want to see happen, not what they have and then visualize that thought until they can feel it. This way, your brain learns to create a new perspective that enables you to become the new you.

Help Others

If possible, try to focus on helping others as a way to take the negative focus off yourself. There is always someone worse than we are. Find groups that support you but also see how you can be there for others. Survivors will tell you how helping, giving, and volunteering make them feel significant in their communities. That is the shift that attracts positive energy into your life. When we make others happy, we feel so glad, but more importantly, our needs happen supernaturally because we extend a hand of generosity.

Try Out Fun New Things

What are the fun things you put off during your painful times? It is time to go back to that passion board and start doing them one after the other. When we are stuck in a bubble, our brain reprograms itself to suit the situation, and to break that label; we must train our brain to do new things. So face your fears and go bungee jumping or skydiving; laugh some more at your mistakes in a cooking class; read stories to kids at your local school. You can volunteer for a Q&A session to teach students the importance of healthy living and use your life as an example. These simple actions will rewire the brain, get you out of your comfort zone, and help you sustain your new self.

I agree that this takes time, but the journey begins when you believe in something new or can be something new. Whatever label we believe in is up to us. If you believe the negative one, then so be it. If you think you can shift that mentality, there is a door waiting for you to walk through something differ- ent. It is genuinely unique what letting go of negativity can do to our lives. It is beyond just healing or recovery.

Many people say they want to heal, but they do not. It doesn't seem to make sense, but they are stuck in that mindset, and as long as they hold on to the past and onto the label, they will never get better. Simple adjustments to your behavior, diet, environment, and stress levels will save you much misery.

If you have symptoms in your body, it's your body yelling at you and screaming at you to do something about it. Everybody I know that has conquered a condition or conquered a disease says it was the best thing that ever happened to them. It changed their life completely. And that's how you have to look at it. You have to look at it like through the lenses of hope, through the lenses of faith, through the confidence that you can take on whatever this challenge is and conquer it and be a better person and a more educated person in the end. There is hope; there are various solutions to overcome your disease and illness without medication or surgery. The possibilities are endless.

Finally, if you missed the chapter titled "Your Support System," goes back and reread it. Some journeys are a walk in the park, while others need a support system. Whether you have friends and family who can be there for you or want to join a support group, go for it. It is a way to meet new people, learn about their stories, share yours, and grow a new mindset.

"You are what you believe in. You become that which you believe you can become"

— BHAGAVAD GITA

18

UNDERSTANDING THE QUANTUM FIELD

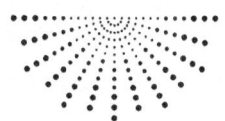

There is something we must all understand about quantum energy healing. The human body might comprise different parts but make no mistakes, as each component work in unison to produce health, wellness, and healing. When we understand this, we will realize the immense capability of the body to heal itself. Natural or holistic healing is a treatment or healing approach that heals the whole body, including where the problem is. This yield better and more effective healing eliminating the adverse effect we do not experience with conventional medication and surgeries.

Additionally, being sick or diseased starts in mind. This is the power of the human consciousness. The mind is a powerful organ capable of alternating our body's energy balance through the thoughts projected to it. If we reprogram our minds to think positively, we can erase the mirage that the mind creates. This way, we alter our current realities about a disease, balance our energies and trigger healing at a spiritual level. This energy balance capability is what quantum healing proposes as an alternative medicine where the body heals itself on its own.

The Power of the Quantum Field Explained

What does the quantum field mean, and how can we use it? We can use it as a tool to manifest anything in our lives. It is an invisible field of energy that carries information. It is the space we cannot see. We are an extension of that field. The human body is a condensed form of energy. We vibrate in and out of that field eight times every second. The fifth dimension exists outside of three-dimensional realities.

Time is infinite. There are endless opportunities. Your desire exists electrically. People keep attracting more of the same things into their lives.

The thoughts come, but the quantum field doesn't respond to what you want. It responds to what you are feeling. If you change how you think and feel, you will send a message to the universe, reprogramming your vibration. If you change your vibration, you change your personality. Our inside world creates our outside world; that is how the quantum field works.

To comprehend this alternative healing modality, you must understand energy. All matter that exists in the universe is made up of energy. We are energetic beings, and as such, we can be healed by rebalancing the power within us. This concept is not new. We can think of ourselves much like a battery. With no energy, we do not function, with strong energy, we work well.

Healing energy technologies and methodologies have existed for centuries, and we are only now returning to them. Why now? There are several reasons. But the main one is the current medical system is failing us. More and more people are seeking alternative ways to heal themselves and others. It is finally time to recognize that we must look at health and healing differently.

Quantum healing is based on the principle that we can self-heal by shifting the energy of our body, mind, and spirit. This can be done by a human being or technology regardless of time or space. Aside from when we are injured by an external force, most ailments begin as emotional issues. For example, unmanaged mental stress can manifest itself as a physical illness. When we address problems at the root cause, we give our body the ability to heal itself. Quantum healing takes the whole person into account, not just the symptom or illness. A growing body of anecdotal evidence suggests this method of healing is comparable to medical science in its potency and is a valid alternative.

Everything Is Energy

$E=mc2$ is the most famous equation in the world, yet modern man and medicine willfully ignore the implications of this remarkable Einstein discovery. In this equation, we see that matter equates to and is essentially made up of energy. You would note that matter is, in essence, organized energy. Information is the organizing principle.

Hence, when looking at biology and medicine, we cannot just look at the biochemical nature of the body. We must also look at the energy and information in the body. Because, at this level of biophysics, the source of health in the body (as well as its deterioration) is clearly evident, properly organized information and energy within the body equate to overall well-being and an "optimal blueprint" for homeostasis and health. When either the information or energy within the body becomes distorted, health deteriorates.

The Simple Truth

Modern medicine has been designed to focus on the Newtonian understanding of physics. This model portrays the world as an intricate mechanism, understanding the human body as a wonderful piece of machinery. Very naturally, if a part of that machinery fails, a method is sought to repair or replace the failed part by supplying the body with tangible aids such as diagnoses, medications, and surgeries, all of which have their place.

But with Einstein came the groundwork for quantum physics, which recognizes that matter at the particle level is energy. This includes what we refer to as the "physical body." As beings of energy, we understand that we are affected by energy.

Health is a clear flow of energy. When your body is harmoniously working and moving at its own pace, you have a high level of energy, which produces happiness, joy, and well-being. In balance, your system works independently from the mind and soul, allowing you to maintain this state for long periods. When you test your bioenergetics field and know how your energy is affected by things in your life, you will be able to take responsibility for the health and wellness of your body and mind.

19

CONCLUSION & OFFER

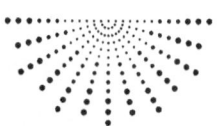

The gift of mental power comes from God, Divine Being, and if we concentrate our minds on that truth, we become in tune with this great power."

— NIKOLA TESLA

I am not a fan of goodbyes, but I know that this book will bring us closer to a lasting relationship about the beautiful power of self-healing and restoring your life force energy. Healing is a difficult journey regardless of the option, but we will attain supernatural healing when we understand that our thoughts, actions, feelings, and surroundings can change.

Throughout this book, I have had one goal in mind: to tell the world that there is healing, natural healing, on the other side, more powerful and effective than you know.

Pharmaceutical companies, our government, and many doctors (not all) will not tell you and don't want you to know. If I have discredited anyone or a profession in any way, that was not my intention. But where doctors may say it's not possible, I say yes it is! We have witnessed, people in hospice got up and left in 2 weeks; people who were paralyzed started walking again, and people who couldn't see, hear or talk can now see, speak and hear. In one month, a stage 4 brain tumor diminished before surgery; Alzheimer's disease stopped and reversed, AIDS and cancer eradicated! Hundreds of COVID-19 victims in the ICU with zero chance of survival, recovered. I see these miracles daily. It is a constant reminder of how powerful our brain, mind, and body are. We cannot forget that we are energetic beings forever connected to source.

Now you know there are other, more powerful options, and it begins by looking at the other side. Over the years, I have grown to understand that human beings are powerful and capable of doing anything, including healing. You can make a difference.

We live in a world where external factors define how healthy we choose to be. So pay attention to your close circle, environment, water, cleaning and beauty products, food, diet, and daily routine, and make that conscious decision to take full responsibility for being healthier than the previous day. You can do it. If the body heals itself, it should make you stronger, healthier, and happier every day.

Please take advantage of the resources and recommendations we have provided here. I have a lifetime of knowledge and experience and am constantly learning about the next best thing. Our clients experience positive outcomes in less than 30 days, regardless of what their doctor tells them. It's time to realize your greatness, step into it, and bring your health and wellness to a new level.

You deserve to live a life free of suffering and pain. You deserve to be free of all disease and illness. It is yours for the taking; all you have to do is make that choice. Thank you for your courage and open-mindedness in reading this book. You are now on the right path to gaining more knowledge, insight, and wisdom toward your healing. I truly wish you nothing but perfect health so that you can enjoy your life full of happiness.

Next Steps:

1.) If you enjoyed this book, please leave an honest review on Amazon.

2.) If you send me a screenshot of your review then you will receive a 30-minute complementary consultation valued at $125.

3.) If you want to learn how we can help you attain that self-healing power, reach out to us through email: **Skye8Angelou@gmail.com**

> **"Even though the body appears to be material, it is not. In the deeper reality, your body is a field of energy, transformation and intelligence."**
>
> — DEEPAK CHOPRA

ABOUT THE AUTHOR

Skye Angelou is a believer in all things possible. Skye also believes that self-healing can be attained under the right conditions. Over 3 decades, the focus has been on restoring, reviving, and rebuilding what was lost to sickness and conventional medicine.

Skye is not your average healer, but a clever, fearless, and spiritual being ready to help facilitate healing for the next person. And could it be you?

Skye Angelou is a beautiful soul that aligns with the universe and happiness from being able to redirect people's disbelief about self-healing to a place where they experience 100% personal health renewal of mind, body, and soul. There is no reason why you cannot enjoy the same level of health as those helped thus far.

Healing is your right. You deserve the right to a healthier, livelier and more fulfilling quality of

life. CLAIM IT NOW! **Connect with Skye today.**
Skye8Angelou@gmail.com